Italy on Two Cappuccinos

Gregory Harris

Italy on Two Cappuccinos

© 2010 by Gregory Harris

All rights reserved. No part of this publication may be reproduced or transmitted in any form or by any means, electronic or mechanical, without written permission from the author, except for brief excerpts used in book reviews.

Disclaimer: It should go without saying that the opinions in this book are strictly my own and are subject to change. Any café, restaurant, museum or other building described may or may not still exist.

Credits: photos were all taken by the author except for Florence (by Yair Haklai) used with Creative Commons Attribution-Share Alike 3.0 Unported license, Ventimiglia (by Patrick Clenet) used with GNU Free Documentation License, Version 1.2, Heilbronn (by P. Schmelzle), used with Creative Commons Attribution Share Alike 2.5 License, Verona by Ern, used with Creative Commons Attribution-Share Alike 2.0 Generic license, and Perugia by Georges Jansoone, used with Creative Commons Attribution 3.0 Unported license. Wow, I thought I had taken more pictures!

Cover photo: *Italy Loves Cappuccino* by Roevin. Used with Creative Commons 2.0 license.

Acknowledgements/Riconoscimenti

I would like to thank my wife Lili for sharing these experiences with me and also for all the happy years since. I also want to thank my mother and the others who read this manuscript and suggested changes (whether I made them or not). *Grazie*, of course, to my friends Andrea and Pedro, without whom this book would have been impossible. Lastly, to the memory of Massimo – *il miglior babbo* – who introduced me to the beauty of Italy as seen through Florentine eyes.

Italy on Two Cappuccinos
A Year in Italy, France and Switzerland

By Gregory Harris

Itinerary

Bologna ... 3
Mantova ... 10
Ferrara ... 13
Castelvetro ... 15
Milano ... 20
Padova ... 25
Verona ... 29
Roma ... 31
Reggello, Vallombrosa ... 40
Firenze ... 41
Lucca ... 44
Lugano ... 51
Lucerne ... 52
Heilbronn ... 54
Angers ... 55
Tours ... 57
Moulins ... 58
Lyons ... 59
Grenoble ... 61
Ventimiglia ... 63
Siena ... 64
Perugia ... 73
Assisi ... 75
Cremona ... 79
Reggio Emilia ... 91
San Gimignano ... 95
Modena ... 100

Introduction

There are a few things you should know before you read the following account. First, living in Italy is very different from vacationing there. We found, living in Modena, that there are myriad customs to get used to that are completely unique to any place you go. As a tourist, these might seem trivial or even quaint, but exposure on a prolonged, daily basis can result in frustration or worse. For example, the daily siesta, from 1:00 – 4:00 (or thereabouts) drove us crazy trying to get things done during our breaks from work, although on a short visit you might not even have time to notice.

Secondly, I read Mark Twain's *Innocents Abroad* just before beginning my own travelogue. If you read it (and I highly recommend it) you will spot my inspiration very quickly and clearly.

Third, I have generally used the Italian names of places, mostly due to the fact that when you're there, that's what you'll see. Most travel books use the local name or both so you shouldn't have any trouble locating the places (should you be so moved).

Prologue

It was 2PM, and we were cold. The town was quiet, and the shops would be closed until 3:30. We had already eaten lunch and finished our walk around the old town and we were now looking for a clean place to warm up and wait for the town to come back to life.

Mantova (Mantua to Shakespeare) is an exceptionally pretty small town, built on a bend in the river Mincio. The Gonzaga dukes ruled from here, and Romeo came here when he was exiled from Verona, just a short drive (or horse ride, I suppose) north. The fortress is part of a large palace complex, including newer palaces and an imposing palazzo on the main square. We were here on a daytrip from our temporary home near Bologna, in the north central region of Italy.

Mantova's narrow medieval streets are filled with locals – during opening hours. Like many of the towns we had visited, we found we could cover the main attractions and then some, at a leisurely pace, in a few hours – which left an awkward gap between a late-morning arrival and an afternoon snack.

Previously, on lazy weekend afternoons in California, we would drink a grande coffee at Starbucks. As in everything Italian, we had to adapt to the local offerings.

"*Due cappucci, per favore*," had replaced our former "double-tall, half-caf, skinny latte" mantra.

The barrista would look again at this pair of...obviously foreigners: no Italian would be drinking a cappuccino at this hour – it was only a breakfast drink for them, never taken at any other time – besides, all good Italians were at home eating lunch with their families now.

He then turned without a word and served up two delicious cappuccinos – just what the doctor ordered.

We lingered over our drinks, savoring the taste, warming our hands and noses before drinking. We observed the people coming and going in the café at this odd hour: two old men who came in to read the sporting news and flirt with the young girl behind the counter; some teenagers done or bored with lunch at home looking for a place to talk away from their parents; a lonely businessman who took his espresso at the counter and left.

An hour later, warm and satisfied, we ventured out again. People were starting to filter back into the cobblestone streets, shops were starting to open, and we had successfully bridged the lunch gap. One day, we thought, some smart Italian will realize that if his shop is open at lunch, he will bring in all the customers who can't shop elsewhere!

This is the story of our lives – or at least the year we spent in Italy, visiting small towns and major cities, what we saw there, and – more importantly – how we survived in Italy on two cappuccinos!

Bologna

Our story starts in Bologna, since it was the first city we visited where we really developed the cappuccino habit. It was still warm in late October when we arrived at the train station, a little lost since we didn't have a map. Arriving in Bologna by car is tricky since the entire center is closed to non-authorized traffic so we thought it best to leave the car at home and train it. On subsequent visits, we did like the Italians and found out that no one ever really cares if you're authorized to drive through the center, or park there, or drive the wrong way down one-way streets as long as you have room to pass. At that time, we were "fresh off the boat" (so to speak) and trying to follow the rules. On subsequent visits, we would park at Porta Saragozza (until some local thugs started charging "protection" money to park there) and walk ten minutes into the Piazza Maggiore.

Arriving by train, we came out of the station and eventually found our way to Via dell'Independenza, a wide, porticoed and café-lined avenue that leads straight to the Fountain of Neptune and the duomo, the heart of the city and one of the most impressive piazzas in Italy.

The duomo, San Petronio, is remarkable for two historical events surrounding it. The first one, you can see as you walk around the building: it's unfinished: the façade is incomplete, you see half-completed Gothic windows, arches without the top, and walls that look chopped off. I couldn't figure out what had happened — an earthquake? WWII bombing? Not quite so sudden, it turns out: the rich Bolognese planners wanted to build the largest church in the world, larger than (the former) St. Peter's in Rome, which had been the largest. They started on that project full bore, until word reached Rome of the plans. The Pope immediately cut the funding for construction and redirected it to build the neighboring Archiginnasio, a handsome, colonnaded university building that runs alongside the church. The architects had to patch up the unfinished church where they could. What remains is still impressive and quite pleasant.

The other event is more significant in its results: Martin Luther, already not a fan of the Church, was appalled by the excesses he saw pouring into the Duomo in Bologna. San

Petronio is credited as being the straw that broke *that* camel's back: after leaving Bologna, Luther went straight back home and wrote his 95 Theses.

Walking clockwise around the interior of the church, I noticed a marble line in the floor with zodiac signs and dates. I found the inscription, which told me that this was the 60th Meridian line, added in 1655 by the astronomer Cassini. The sun comes in through a hole in the ceiling (watch where you sit if it's raining on Sunday!) and falls along the line. The spot where it hits at noon tells you the date and zodiac sign. This is the curious mix of science and religion you find in unexpected places all over Italy.

We also noticed a large number of students on the steps in front of the church. Which means the Archiginnasio is still a university building and that made me feel better: this wasn't just a tourist trap, real people actually come here and sit.

Leaving the duomo, we crossed the piazza to the Palazzo Comunale, originally built in the 14th century with additions from the 15th, 16th and 17th. The building is quite impressive and takes up the better part of a city block. The styles, while different, somehow work together. The oldest part of the building has crenellations along the top and a clock tower on the corner.

We wandered in, just to see what we could see and it was a small bonanza. Up the wide staircase (it's that wide because horse-drawn carriages used to go up this way – I'm not kidding) we found a museum through one door, and offices through another. We wandered through the office door and admired the art inside, the frescoed walls, paintings and plaques everywhere. There are also many rooms where you can enter without paying admission. The most important of these is the main salon, in which Napoleon announced the independence of Bologna from the Papal States. That probably wasn't the independence the Bolognese had in mind, however, as they simply came under Napoleon's rule. At any rate, there's a gift shop at the end, and we got some great photos out of those windows.

Back outside, it's impossible to miss the Fountain of Neptune. It's a large bronze fountain, with an imposing naked Neptune standing above four nude sirens who symbolize the four continents known at that time (or the four seas, or the four major rivers or the four winds – it changes depending on who you ask). They (the sirens, that is) are holding their breasts, which are spurting water.

I've often thought what the reaction must have been when this statue was unveiled some 500 years ago. I mean, here's a very public statue with larger than life nudes in provocative poses, never mind the subject matter is supposedly classical Greco-Roman. It's being introduced to a society that has only recently been released from 1000 years of Church domination, during which time the slightest "impure" thought was a punishable offense, and art, when it existed at all, was a depiction of the

Bible or of a religious scene, very strict and very pious.

Then came the Renaissance, a celebration of the human form and intellect. The change must have been huge, and the introduction of nude statues to a public that had been told this was sinful must have been quite confusing. Of all the works I've seen, this fountain is definitely one of the more – how should I say – brazen when it comes to its display of nudity and the poses of the characters. How can you explain to children that it's wrong to run around naked when this is what they see, smack in the middle of the town's main square? Nevertheless, it is an impressive sculpture, and this Neptune's trident is known around the world today for its appearance on the grille of every Maserati: the Maserati brothers started here before moving to Modena to make their famous sports cars.

We've stopped at a number of cafés in Bologna, and they have all been...just OK. Not bad, but not great, nothing to write home about. However, we've never made it to the intriguing Café Nutella on Via Independenza, and it's possible that it or its neighbors would change my mind.

On the other hand, we've been hard pressed to have a bad meal here. The best, I think, was the first, in a rustic trattoria off the Piazza San Francesco. For some reason we haven't been back even though we walk past it often. It has simple wooden chairs and tables on a wood floor. The front is open and there are two rooms with maybe six tables each. The menu is the same as you'll find in any restaurant in central Italy: pasta and more pasta, maybe a pork dish or two and grilled veggies or a salad. We both ordered our pastas with the local specialty, *al ragù*, which we call Bolognese (meat sauce) back home. It was rich and tasty with pieces of beef, not acidic with ground beef like I've had back home.

One night, after dinner with friends, we found the best gelato in Bologna. We had walked through the medieval streets north of Ugo Bassi, the main thoroughfare, through the former ghetto and by even more medieval towers. We finally came out in a long, well-lit piazza with a hotel and, across the street, an uninviting dive with a long line in front. The place had no sign to speak of. The fluorescent lighting was harsh and dim and the women behind the counter were unsmiling and brusque but you practically had to buy a ticket just to get in. The flavors here were wild mixes (well, wild by Italian standards) of various flavors (generally chocolate, cream and Nutella) but there were also some fruit flavors made with real fruit. The prices were lower than most gelato we've seen and once we were finally served we had to admit that the wait had been worth it.

By the time we left it was past midnight, the night was cooling down quite a bit and people were still showing up. On our way past the San Francesco church, we noticed that there was a fair-sized gathering on the grass in front of the church. Several dozen students and young people were hanging out here, playing guitar, drinking, talking and necking. It turns out this is their space away from parents. We finally reached the car and drove home, amazed as usual at the number of cars on the road at 1:00 AM on weeknights.

Mantova

The approach to Mantova is quite dramatic. We were following the signs, and knew we were close. But now we were driving along a typical 2-lane road through forested countryside, not seeing anything like a city around us. After a while, we hit a bend in the road and there it was, smack in front of us across a wide river, all towers and spires, a large fortress prominently in the foreground. There's no time to stop and admire the view, though: you're at a bridge and have to drive towards the fortress. It must have been quite impressive from horseback. On the other side of the river, we parked along the bank and we walked into the town.

When we came back here in the summer, we went down the bank to the river instead. There was a beer garden there and a promenade along the river. We also found a way into the palace complex: we walked down the driveway to the museum, then from there into a private courtyard and from there we made our way to the gardens. When I say gardens, what I mean is a lawn with trees. Nevertheless, it was a very pleasant courtyard, even in winter. From there we walked out through the palazzo ducale into Piazza Sordello.

Mantova is a city of attractive architecture, with one piazza leading to the next through almost the entire old town. In the summer months, these piazzas overflow with tables and chairs from the numerous *gelaterie*, restaurants, *pizzerie* and cafes that line them. The most touristy of these are in Piazza Sordello, which is the large square bordered by the imposing palace, the duomo and the archbishop's palace. The drinks here are overpriced and served by uncaring waitresses who don't understand *la dolce vita*. At least the people-watching is good – we stayed an hour watching the crowds go by, walking from one piazza to the next.

There are always vendors selling clothing, art and old junk they call antiques in the arcades of Piazza dell'Erbe, the one with the medieval clock tower. On our first visit here, a bone-chilling wind was blowing through the piazzas and we were extremely happy to find a woman selling hats and gloves. They made an excellent souvenir. In the summer we returned and bought sunglasses. San Lorenzo, a round brick (decommissioned) church next to the medieval brick clock tower, looked so intriguing and ancient from the outside that we just had to see inside. That was a waste of time and money. We spent all of 10 minutes seeing all the fragments of frescoes the place had to offer. It was a mistake we rarely make, since we usually look at the postcards first.

We sat down at a couple of restaurants in the Piazza dell'Erbe which were reasonably priced and quite pleasantly located although the service and food (unfortunately) left something to be desired.

We also found a small river that surfaces for a block then flows between charming medieval houses while you stand on what is technically a covered bridge but feels more like a porticoed sidewalk.

The short walk along the bank is quite pleasant, and provides some views of houses along the banks that make you want to live here. This is not to be confused with the promenade along the Mincio, however. That is a long path through a green park along the riverbank. In nice weather, this is the place to be. There are also beer gardens and boat rides here.

Our favorite café in Mantova (closed on Sundays) is off the beaten path, in its own little piazza. With Sant'Andrea at your back, turn right on Via Verdi until you come to a piazza on your right. You'll see a large, detached building sitting at the end, with tables outside in the summer and in an enclosed area in the winter. The décor is, inexplicably, 1920s sporty (yachting, tennis, boxing, and jazz). On a dark winter night, the cappuccino here is large and tasty and in the summer a refreshing drink (inside or out) is just right.

Ferrara

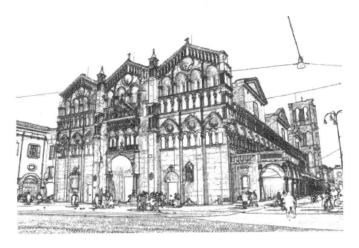

A few weeks later, we set out for another destination, not too far from Mantova, or from home, for that matter: Ferrara, former capital of the Estense Dukes before they moved their capital to Modena. Although the city has only 180,000 inhabitants, its broad avenues and crowded, busy historic center make it feel much larger.

It was still cold when we visited Ferrara. In fact, it was close to the middle of December but this time we were prepared with coats, hats, scarves, and gloves. What we were not prepared for was the labyrinth of streets around the city center, many of which are (theoretically) closed to traffic or cars without a permit. All told, it probably took us half an hour to park, and then we ended up in a metered space – which I hate when exploring since you have to remember to get back to the car, and how to get back to the car, in order to move it or feed the meter some hours later.

We had planned on walking around and seeing a few sights: the cathedral, the castle, and the statues in the main piazza, then grabbing a bite to eat, but now that we were here, we reversed the plans and decided to eat first. We found a small place just outside the center where the owner and his wife fed us like family with freshly made pasta. Oh, and beer (for me), Diet Coke (shudder) for Lili, no cappuccino just yet – the atmosphere in this place wasn't right (well, it wasn't a café), and we were saving our caffeine fix for an afternoon break – it wouldn't do to have a cappuccino just anywhere. We're not promiscuous or gratuitous drinkers.

The center of Ferrara won't disappoint even the most jaded traveler. The placement of the buildings around the squares, the marble and brick, and the imposing, unexpected, moated castle right in the thick of things is the stuff fairy tales are made of. Even better, right across from the cathedral and its complicated, Romanesque façade, and just around the corner from the castle, was a large, elegant café with a glassed-in patio. Bingo! We didn't succumb, though. Not right away. First we did what we had come for: we crossed the moat and toured the castle – the parts that were free, anyway –

how often do you get to walk undisturbed along the parapets of an old castle, overlooking an actual moat, pretending to be one of the old dukes? You think about the extremely large Spanish cannon planted outside, the white-washed, drafty hallways inside, the dark dungeon below and the towers above with a view over the entire town.

There are actually a few cafes lining the piazza from the castle to the street and there's even a McDonald's for the cultural imperialists in town. It's guarded by the police during opening hours. The café you choose is a matter of personal preference, of course – but we prefer large, well-lit places with lots of seating. The service is friendly in these places and the coffee, despite the location, is quite cheap at the counter. In the summer, there are tables on the sidewalk under awnings and umbrellas. The piazza is lively and makes for a relaxing break.

Castelvetro

Castelvetro is a tiny little town in Modena province (if it's in Modena province, you *know* it's small). We went one bright Sunday in December when we had only an afternoon to explore. The drive, through a few low hills and what undeveloped countryside exists in Emilia Romagna, was pleasant, with the snow, an already unusual occurrence, covering the fields and rooftops. Castelvetro is built on one of these hills, so its spires and walls are visible from a distance.

Driving up, you can't tell how small it is until you are halfway up the hill and realize that you're already in it. We did just that and found ourselves on the hilltop in no time. We parked in the first space we saw, which happened to be in Piazza Roma. Piazza Roma is less impressive than it sounds: it is a modest piazza, perched on the side of the stone face of the hill, now given over to (a maximum of 8) parking spaces. There was a medieval watchtower there, with Christmas lights running up the corners. The view from the piazza was great, with a commanding view of the valley as well as the city walls. The balcony on the palazzo pubblico overlooked this piazza and this must have been the social center of town.

Since it was Sunday, the town was closed and quiet and we took a short walk around before it got too cold. The center of the town, we found, is tiny and walkable in 15 minutes, if you take your time and carefully study each building. Still, the old houses were very pretty and well maintained; the public buildings were impressive but not overpowering. The single church turned out to be an early 20th century reproduction of something they wish they had built earlier, but it was very clean and tasteful – except for the fiber-optic, kaleidoscopic flowers in front of a statue of the Madonna. The visit to the church stretched our stay by maybe two and a half minutes. Walking out, we looked around for the next attraction. There were two choices: the town store and the bar, directly across from the church.

To say the town was closed is a little misleading, actually. After all, there is only one shop there. I was disappointed but not surprised to find it closed on Sunday, since it looked like an old-fashioned general store, selling local jams and rustic-looking artwork.

The bar, on the other hand, was open and so we decided to investigate. The door gave no indication of what might be expected inside, and we were quite surprised. We walked into a moderate sized room dominated by the bar, with four small tables taking up the remainder of the space. There were two rooms off this one, however, and there was the trick to the place's popularity: the entire town population was sequestered here. One room was a video game room, and it was filled with what looked like Castelvetro's entire teen population. The other door led to a room filled with large round tables, all of them full of elderly men playing cards. There was a further room off of this one, with a large (for Italy) TV placed like a movie screen, and about two dozen chairs placed in rows to watch sporting events or maybe the odd video.

So we had found the secret to Castelvetro: everyone, and every age, had their place in the town bar. With one exception. It took me a few minutes to notice, but I finally realized that, despite the obvious popularity of this place, there were no women here: none drinking coffee, none playing cards, and certainly none playing arcade games. The women, we realized, were home cooking lunch, while the men and the children socialized.

I had to wonder what I would be thinking if I were one of those girls, still young enough to be playing games and flirting with boys. Were they getting the most out of life now, before they, too, ended up in the kitchen while their husbands and kids had all the fun? Were they jealous, accepting, rebelling, apathetic, or fatalistic? It wasn't until several months later that I asked some Italian girls that question. The answer I got was that they really didn't think about it: that was life, they would cook for their husbands in time, and that was that. Hadn't it always been that way? In our last week there another friend explained it to me this way: Europeans tend to view history as a weight to bear, while Americans see it as a springboard. "It's always been that way" is an obligation to Europeans – none more so than Italians, who live in a glorious past of emperors and artists – while it is a challenge to Americans to progress, to break the mold and move beyond what's always been done. There are certainly benefits to both points of view but I can't really say one is better than the other.

We ordered our cappuccinos from the unsmiling but efficient barrista, who didn't say anything except the price. Cheaper than Modena, but then this wasn't an historic piazza or a dazzling historic café, either. We found a free table (one of the two) and sat down to watch the locals and warm up.

Outside the town hall and in the alcove by the church we saw posters advertising a concert in the church that night. We toyed with the idea of sticking around, but figured we would go crazy looking for something to do around here for five hours.

Instead, we stopped at the bottom of the hill where a small river was covered in ice. There was a pedestrian bridge over it and we walked across and tromped in the snow for a while, while the sun was out and looked up at the small but impressive skyline the town's towers and walls gave from here, the steep hill giving it a more forbidding look that it really possessed.

Milano

Locals call Milan "a city to discover." What they mean by that is, there is nothing about Milan that is obviously attractive and the little that there is must be teased out, detail by detail, over time. If you plan on living here, that's probably OK: you can spend all day every day looking for those hidden gems and secret gardens. I remember, when I was 18, being in Italy on an art history tour. We drove through Milan, driving by the duomo. We slowed down as the teacher pointed to it (not that he needed to), explaining, that is the Duomo, started in the 14th century but not finished until Napoleon took over, and that the building is covered with over 3000 statues. Then we left Milan.

I didn't understand why we didn't stop and see more until this year.

There is, in fact, more to see in Milan, and the best part is that it is all in a line, from the Duomo through the Galleria Vittorio Emanuele (don't stop to shop or eat here, no one does – just walk through – step on the bull's testicles if you must) to La Scala and on to Via della Spiga, the street famous for its haute couture boutiques. On a good day, this can take you 30 minutes, more if you stop in each boutique. Once you have made your way down the few blocks to where the tour buses park, you're done and you can move on.

It was Sunday afternoon when we were there and every shop on the Via della Spiga was, of course, closed. Except for a bar we found. It looked very swank: blue walls, gilt ceiling, chandeliers and an old-fashioned wood bar. I was afraid it would be pricey but in fact it was quite reasonable. The reason was that the coffee was just OK, but I think this location is more for the see-and-be-seen crowd than for coffee lovers. The caffeine shot propelled us back to the Duomo, anyway although I couldn't figure out why we wanted to be back there in a swarm of tourists, immigrants, souvenir hawkers and pigeons.

Aside from the few central blocks mentioned above, Milan is filled with modern architecture. What passes for modern architecture in Italy is generally an insult to sensibility. Especially painful are the buildings that mock (some more forgiving minds might say *mimic*) the medieval arcaded buildings with squared off marble and concrete tapered "arcades" and even the occasional overhanging upper story. These buildings are harsh and angular, and fall short of the mark of impressive or grand that the originals give. I have found that the best way to approach these modern buildings is looking down.

Perhaps the most offensive building I have seen (and I am measuring the amount of offense by its sheer size and visibility, not because it is the absolute worst, although it is close) is the Torre Velasca, a towering postwar mixed use affair, visible from every part of the city. The top 10 or so floors overhang the lower 30, with long slabs of concrete sticking diagonally up, perversely mirroring a square medieval castle turret. The effect is ponderous and top-heavy. What's more, the bottom floors get even less light than they would normally due to the overhang and the multiple concrete supports. As is typical of this style, those who live inside look out over a beautiful view of the city, completely unaware of the blight their building creates for all the other views.

We had caught glimpses of this building walking around the town, but it was from the roof of the duomo that we had an uninterrupted view of it, blocking a good portion of the city beyond. (If you have the chance, and money is no object, head up to the roof of the Duomo for some nice views: rooftops are the nicest view of Milan and you can take impressive photos.)

"What is *that*?" I asked the guard, pointing at the thing. I need not have pointed; he knew exactly what I meant.

"La Torre Velasca," he responded, his face expressionless. "Apartments on top, offices below." It seemed he was none too fond of the place, either. We turned to look the other way.

Oh, sorry there is one other thing to see in Milan, and that is Leonardo's Last Supper. Yes, that one. The challenge, of course, is to actually see it: to show up and buy a ticket is not sufficient, first you must call ahead to get a reservation to buy a ticket. If you're in town for a day, forget it: it's best to call a week ahead to get your half-hour window (well, an Italian half hour – bring a good book).

Things weren't always this way. Mark Twain, when he came here, wrote about his visit to the monastery to see this famous fresco. It was free then – in fact, they had trouble getting people to come at all. I was fascinated to learn that the Renaissance was considered a bad time for art by the Italians of the mid 19th century, and even more surprised to learn that this incredibly famous work was almost lost thanks to a combination of neglect and horses – by the time Napoleon got here, the painting was already badly deteriorated, so he had no qualms about using the room as a stable for his horses.

According to Twain, the horses kicked off most of the fresco below the knees. Well, Twain's account was according to those telling it to him, so there may be some exaggeration there – Italy was also in the midst of a civil war for unification and it's just possible that someone besides the French contributed to the damage. It's easy to see why they're so angry with the French: the Italians (*read* Caesar) brought the light of civilization to France (*read* invaded Gaul) just a few years ago (*read* 18 centuries before). Those barbarians (*read* Napoleon) repaid the favor by stealing (*read* well, OK he stole) the best art in the world (*read* the Mona Lisa and other Da Vinci paintings) and displaying it in some monstrosity of a building (*read* The Louvre). And they've held that animosity ever since.

Lastly, I should mention that there are some well-regarded museums here, including the Pinacoteca (picture gallery) and the Modern Art Museum. Regrettably, my allergy to museums and lack of a disposable face mask kept us away. Visit at your own risk: a bomb went off in front of the latter in the early '90s in protest of... what, you think they needed a reason? You've been warned.

Padova

Padova, or Padua, is too close to Venice for its own good. Tourists in the know can take advantage of this fact, finding reasonable accommodations and a city relatively undiscovered by the unwashed masses that throng Venice. Padova is certainly worth the visit if only for the frescoes by Giotto in the Scrovegni chapel, or the Basilica of Saint Anthony. These two items alone (or together) should convince anyone within a half-hour radius (i.e. visiting Venice) that Padova is really worth the visit.

We arrived in Padova in the late afternoon. It was after lunch and everything was open again. We didn't really come to Padova to see it. You see, it was Carnival season in Venice, so we really wanted to go *there*. We came to Padova to find a convenient jumping-off point, since

Venice was not only a madhouse but fully booked. Besides, the hotels in Venice are so small...why stay there when you can stay down the road for half the price and get much more pleasant accommodations to boot?

We were feeling flush and confident as we drove in, despite almost getting lost once or twice thanks to the importune placement of the old city walls. I thought perhaps it was time to live high on the hog, as it were, so I chose a nice hotel from my Michelin guide. One looked especially promising, on the main road but quite close to the old town. I stopped and walked in, Michelin Guide in hand – which had the opposite effect of what I was looking for: the proprietor immediately raised his prices. I showed him the rate in the book, and he showed me his fuzzy math that translated Lire into Euros at a very advantageous rate, explaining that the costs had gone up since the guide had been published (earlier this year), but he would be glad to give me a discount anyway. He mentioned a rate somewhere between the guide's prices and his original quote. Since there was no room for negotiation, and we had been looking to stay in a nice hotel anyway, we accepted.

I won't bore you with the details of the hotel; suffice it to say that the room was fairly well-appointed. In the early 1970s.

Walking through the old town we discovered a discreet, luxury hotel nestled off an arcaded walk with barely a sign suggesting its presence. One look inside told me we had erred in taking the room at our – by way of comparison – faded and soulless hotel.

This brings me to my biggest beef with the Michelin Guide: these people think they can set up their own rating system for every hotel and restaurant! In Italy especially, the Michelin ratings have no apparent bearing on the number of stars the hotel may have. Sometimes this is a good thing, as there may be any number of...let's say *eager* government officials willing to add a star or two in exchange for a free room or a kickback. Michelin, on the other hand, has a vested interest in being honest and neutral: if they are unreliable, people won't buy their guides. Or so goes the theory. Still, perhaps they could tell you why they disagree with the stars on the hotel itself, which would make things so much simpler.

But I digress. The point is that Padova was a pleasant surprise. We walked around the old market, built in the 13th century, which was bustling still, some 800 years later. We also walked through here at night, in an eerie fog, which was almost like being in a time warp.

Padova is home to San Antonio of Texan renown and his basilica is a major pilgrimage destination. I'm not much of a pilgrim, but I wanted to see what the fuss was all about and I was not disappointed. Inside the very large, unusually domed building was a well-planned interior. We perambulated along the pilgrimage track, looking at the chapels and tombs along the walls. We also stopped to see the black Madonna here, but she just seemed a little dirty to me. Apparently there are a number of these Madonnas around Europe which are of special interest to conspiracy buffs, among others.

Padova is also home to Caffè Pedrocchi. It is a large, multiroom affair that opened in 1831 and has remained open since. Not quite as much a pilgrimage as San Antonio, this is still well worth a stop to follow in the footsteps of Stendahl and Lord Byron. We tried, but the night we were there, there was a private party for Carnevale and the café was closed to the general public.

Despite my allergy, we did enter a museum here: the one attached to the Cappella degli Scrovegni, an intimate chapel painted by Giotto who left his mark all over town but really knocked one out of the park here. The history of the chapel is interesting: Enrico Scrovegni, who commissioned the chapel, is supposedly the son of a character that Dante met in the seventh circle of hell. Did Enrico build the chapel with that in mind? Oh, you should also know that, just like the Last Supper in Milano, you need to buy tickets in advance. Unless you're a pretty girl (or traveling with one) who can charm the ticket vendor on a slow day – we got our tickets and waited only an Italian half hour to get in. I'm pretty hard to please but I was happy that we did it.

Verona

Like Padova, and close to it, Verona was a pleasant surprise off the typical tourist route, but still visitor-friendly. Most people know Verona as the home of Romeo and Juliet, and you can visit Juliet's house and see the balcony of Romeo's famous speech. Of course, Romeo and Juliet is a fictional work, and Shakespeare never visited Verona, so this is really just a silly tourist attraction. Nevertheless, we went and took pictures and rubbed Juliet's breast for good luck (she's a bronze statue).

From there we strolled through the nearby Piazza delle Erbe, with its old frescoed houses, fountain and statues. The piazza reminded me of Piazza San Marco in Venice for the enclosed nature of the square and the lion on the statue. It was a pleasant place to stop and watch the people with a nice cappuccino at one of the numerous cafés.

We crossed the Ponte Scaligero, which is a crenellated medieval bridge attached to the Castelvecchio (old castle) which is apparently filled with nice art. From there, it is a healthy walk through historic but nondescript streets to the basilica of San Zeno, which is considered one of the great Romanesque churches. The outside consists of a mismatched façade, old brick tower and "new" bell tower. Inside, the building is light and pleasant for an old church. I thought it looked like a zebra, with its odd striped pattern, which made me want to call it San Zebra. We attached ourselves discreetly to a tour group going through to get the lowdown on the history of the place.

From here, we walked along the river back to the town's other attractions, and closer to our destination, the Roman amphitheater, the Arena of Verona, located off a piazza with the unlikely name of Brà.

Smaller than the Coliseum in Rome, Verona's Arena has the benefit of still being intact and, even better, performances are still given here in the summer. We found the box office and picked up tickets for Bizet's Carmen. The arena has excellent acoustics despite its size, so you can hear the whole performance from any seat without microphones. When I say seat, I am using that term loosely since there are, of course, no seats here. The Romans built long stone benches, and this is what you sit on. The Italians have arranged this so you squish as close to your neighbor as you can and try not to kick the person sitting in front of you. For a modest fee, you can buy a pillow and I'd recommend that for any show over one hour because that stone gets pretty hard. The arena is quite large, and the spectacle of seeing a show in this setting was hard to beat. We left (4½ hours later) ecstatic, if a little sore and cramped.

Roma

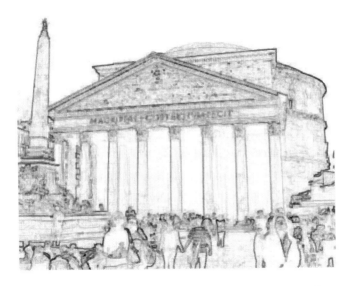

Mark Twain said, during his visit here in 1865, that true joy lies in discovery. And therefore he would not be joyful in Rome since there is absolutely nothing to discover here.

What he said then is even truer today, although (ironically) he never saw the Roman Forum since it was underground until Mussolini had it unearthed and the glory of Rome once again displayed. Whereas you might visit some untouristed city like Padova or Bologna and enjoy the thrill of seeing a gem that only locals had seen, in Rome you can only gawk at what countless millions of others have seen, are seeing with you and will see after you. That's not to say it's not pretty or that there is nothing worth seeing: just that what you see will not be a revelation. The Coliseum, the Sistine Chapel, the Trevi fountain and the Spanish Steps are all so iconic, ingrained in our collective consciousness that you feel more like you are seeing an old friend rather than discovering a foreign city.

So what did we do in Rome? First we found a hotel. Not a big problem, you might think, there are easily enough hotels in Rome to handle the millions of tourists who come for major occasions. We thought that coming in early March, with no major holidays in sight, would give us a quiet "Roman Holiday" style weekend, with the city empty of (other) tourists. Wrong! Apparently about three million other people, from every country in the world, had the same idea and had all descended on Rome for this same weekend. The train station was packed. The subway was packed. The hotel we had chosen (sight-unseen, which I almost never do) had one room left – for a price worthy of New York City in a room about the same size as you would find there. It was quaint and central, though, so we didn't complain. Plus, we would only be here one night. At the hotel, we remarked that it seemed awfully busy for an off-weekend. The clerk told us that no, it was like this year-round.

The hotel was in spitting distance of the Vatican, and we also realized that Sunday would be the first Sunday of the month, meaning the museums were free. We made plans to be in line early: we would not be the only ones there. More on that visit later.

Next, we tried to hook up with an American friend who lived in Rome with his Italian fiancée and with an American couple who were also in town this weekend. The moral of the story is that you cannot bring together three groups with different agendas inside 48 hours.

We did meet up with the local couple, which was great: they showed us around and took us places tourists wouldn't normally have found (no, I won't tell you where we went). I will tell you that we met at the Pantheon (which is definitely worth seeing) and walked to Piazza Navona.

The Pantheon is considered the best example of Roman architecture still standing and it is indeed amazing that it is still standing considering the drubbing every other Roman building in Rome got over the years. I won't go into detail about its history or its "perfect" dimensions, since every art history textbook covers that – like I said, there is nothing new in Rome. What I will say is that walking around inside is taking a trip through a time machine. Not with one single stop but with several stops: the last 2000 years have left their marks on the one-time temple, and each of them is worth examining.

More striking than the interior is the way the Pantheon appears to be sunken in the ground today. The buildings all around are built on a slope that goes up from the temple so that if you were to level the ground, you would bury the Pantheon. Which goes to show just how far Rome has come up over the years: the forum is equally well below street level. As buildings fell down, new buildings were built on top, forming layers of strata, each one signaling an era. There are apparently at least four layers of ruins under present-day Rome: medieval Rome, Christian Rome, post-Nero Rome, and pre-Imperial Rome. It was always a trip to consider the amount of history you are walking on here, even in the most banal souvenir shop.

Piazza Navona is one of the more popular places in Rome with both locals and tourists, for good reason. The piazza is large with a pleasant atmosphere. There are baroque buildings that have just recently been cleaned – in the guidebooks, they appear rust-colored, but now they are off-white. There are dozens of cafés and restaurants, and crowds of people who are just here to see and be seen. There are the usual tourist traps and souvenir stands, but there is also a genuine atmosphere here of sophistication, joie de vivre Roman-style and entertainment. Altogether a great place to be, especially as the day turns to night.

I know, I know, I keep telling you that I am allergic to museums. And it's true. Every time I go to one, the allergy becomes a little stronger. Such was the experience at the Vatican museum on that free Sunday. I figured, this is one of the premier museums in the world, might as well take advantage of the fact that we're here and it's free. The hotelier warned us to get there early to beat the crowds; he even offered to make us an early breakfast at 7:00. We laughingly declined, figuring we would get to the museum at 9:00, an hour before it opened, and be towards the front of the line, no problem.

We skidded up to the Vatican a few minutes past 9:00, and had no problem at all identifying the entrance to the museum: it was the one with the line in front of it, about four people wide and a mile or so long. Again, what might have been a good theory in a less popular place turned out to be the same plan that some 10,000 other people had that morning. Nothing to do now but get in line. Still, we were lucky that we got here when we did: the line doubled in length over the next hour.

We managed to get in around half past ten, and the museum had yet to reach capacity. I had no desire to see yet more religious painting, so we made a dash for the Sistine Chapel, which neither of us had seen in its restored state. And here, I would like to add a hint for any of you who plan on visiting this place: the Vatican museums are set up in a circuit: you really can't deviate from it, something it would have been nice to know before going in. We ran through the galleries to get to the chapel, which becomes unpleasantly crowded quickly. We skipped the exhibits along the way, none of which we wanted to see, except the Raphael rooms, which were open today (they're usually closed). These are the rooms that Raphael had frescoed with some of the most recognizable paintings of his career: *The School of Athens*, with Michelangelo and Leonardo as Plato and Aristotle, etc. We figured we would see the Sistine Chapel and loop back later when the crowds were in the chapel.

I am happy to say that the first part of my theory worked: the Sistine Chapel was fairly uncrowded at that hour and it was worth the wait and the dash to see it like this. At this time, we could move around at our own pace, examining the famous ceiling, and stepping up close to the walls to examine the details. The colors were vibrant, more alive than anyone had expected from the Renaissance: bright orange, lime green, all shades of red and blue.

Like most of the others in the room, we had brought our guidebook. If you are like me, you hate to walk around with one of these anchors, but even I realized it was well worth the effort to carry one here. Otherwise, you miss out on a lot of the patterns and symbols in the paintings and the who and why of each. We spent a good 45 minutes here, just enjoying. When the crowds started to come in, and we had seen enough, we left through the only exit, a tiny door that leads to a staircase. Then came the hard part: backtracking. It was at this point that we realized the museum was set up as a circuit, and to get back to anything you have already seen you have to go to the beginning and start again (without the line or the metal detector, at least).

By this time it was close to noon and the place was filling up with all the late risers. By the time we got close to the Raphael rooms, we could barely move. I was getting claustrophobic, and we still had to follow an outdoor walkway, some more stairs, and more hallways. I was still optimistic that not everyone would be going through the Raphael rooms: there were signs to the Sistine chapel that might siphon off a good deal of the hoi polloi. Only later did I realize that it was all part of the circuit and everyone was on the same path, regardless of the signs.

The only way to the Sistine chapel was through the Raphael rooms. I'm not sure how they managed that, or how we managed to skip them on our first pass. It was poor planning on the Vatican's part to direct the crowds this way, as many people really only wanted to see the Sistine Chapel and didn't really give a hoot about Raphael, or had only a passing interest. So the rooms had two opposing currents: those who wanted to see the rooms and those who were merely passing through. There was also a subcurrent of people passing through who decided to stop and look around, too. I was getting really crazy at this point and my nerves were fraying. There were too many people: I couldn't enjoy the walls, as much as I wanted to see them. We were being jostled and pushed and moved by the currents. I was also getting really hungry since we had skipped breakfast to gain some time. So I got an eyeful of the place and then escaped to snack on my smuggled food in the bathroom.

When I got out, Lili and I were hopelessly separated, and there was nothing for it but to head for the exit...which was through the Sistine Chapel, now completely mobbed and impassable. Just getting here, through the winding, too-narrow passages and the stairs and the crowds, took a while. Trying to move across the packed floor of the place was draining and irritating, everyone still pushing and fighting for space. The ceiling and the walls brought no joy this time, no sense of wonder. I fought for the exit, where I had to wait: the door was simply too small for the mass of people trying to circulate through, and the crowds were pushing from behind. It took another half hour to get through the crowds in the halls and to finally make it to the exit. I got outside the building and sat on the curb, waiting for Lili. I was drained. She finally made it out, also exhausted and hungry. We sat down at the first restaurant we found and ate reheated spaghetti (*mental note:* never eat anywhere near the tourist attractions in Rome if you want to actually enjoy the food). We had had enough of museums for another twelve months.

Before leaving Rome, we visited a fantastic little church called San Clemente. This attractive church was built in the 12th century, which makes it pretty old, even by Roman standards. However, what makes it even more interesting is that it was built on top of an older, fourth century church, which you can still visit. And that church, in turn, is built on top of a temple to Mithras, the leading religion in Rome before the rise of Christianity. That temple was destroyed by the Christians erecting the church, but one room still remains pretty much intact and is open for visits. The sound of rushing water is supposedly the original Roman sewer, the cloaca maxima. I have heard that, since our visit, other Roman apartments and perhaps even the house of St. Clement (the eponymous saint of the basilica) have been excavated on the same level as the pagan temple, which must make this visit down through time even more amazing than it was when we were there.

We stopped at a café across the street from the church and enjoyed a rich cappuccino, while watching locals and tourists, schoolchildren and old men mixing on the sidewalk.

Reggello, Vallombrosa

Some of the nicest places are the small villages that you might pass through without even knowing there is something there – again, Mark Twain's theory of the joy in discovery. Reggello and Vallombrosa are two such towns, south of Florence, almost unmarked and hard to get to from the Autostrada. Both towns are in the hilly country of Tuscany, on roads that snake through the forests. There is nothing too spectacular about either, just pleasant little places where nothing much happens and hiking in the rosemary-covered hills is the order of the day.

A coffee in the only café in Vallombrosa was quite enjoyable – despite the owner's accent. The typical Tuscan accent, aspirating the letter "C" between two vowels, makes a traditional *cappuccino con cacao* sound more like a Coca Cola and it took me a few tries to get what I wanted. There is a hotel in Vallombrosa, if the term "hotel" isn't being too generous. I mention it not because the rooms aren't anything to write home about, but the restaurant makes the tastiest *bistecca fiorentina* I've ever tasted.

Firenze

Firenze, or Florence, is such a famous city that it's hard to write about. In fact, so many books have been written about Florence and there are so many famous names attached to it that I will content myself with just skimming the cream. We visited here many times with Andrea and Cinzia and their friends. Florence is divided into several parts, but mostly there's the tourist-filled center where everything worth seeing lies, and the areas outside that which are fairly nondescript but where the food is better.

Most of the historic center of Florence worth seeing is found within a few blocks along the Via Calzaioli, from the Duomo to the Ponte Vecchio over the Arno river. This area is therefore the most crowded but also contains the places you have to see.

It's true that we owe the Renaissance to Florentine artists and patrons, and probably a good deal of modern trade and government, too. So it's worth coming to see where all that went down, 500 years ago.

To be sure, there are plenty of things to see that are not along the Via Calzaioli, but it is the best place to start. The Duomo is probably the most impressive façade you are likely to come across, with its bold reds and greens and Brunelleschi's impossibly large dome. If it's open, it's absolutely worth the climb to the top. By contrast, the interior feels strangely hollow. The baptistery doors by Ghiberti and other artists are sublime works of artistry that are almost unmatched to this day in their execution.

Walking further down the road, past gelaterie and the market, you will come to the Palazzo Vecchio or old palace, best known today as the home of the Medici dukes. The sculptures on display in the Piazza della Signoria are mostly replicas of the originals – to see Michelangelo's original David today, head to the Galleria dell'Accademia a few blocks away. To see even more art, hit the just famous Uffizi Gallery around the corner.

If you keep on going, you will cross the Ponte Vecchio, or old bridge, now almost sinking under the weight of tourists and crammed with jewelers. Most of these shops are licensed, so if you're looking for a unique souvenir, you could do worse than stopping in. Once you cross the bridge, you notice that the impressive buildings taper off quickly, leaving only the Palazzo Pitti with its Boboli Gardens.

Two of my favorite sites in Florence are the church and piazza of Santa Croce, which, in contrast to the Duomo is almost modest on the outside but intricate and beautiful on the inside.

It's hard to recommend cafés here since we avoided most of them. Suffice it to say that the farther you get from the Via Calzaioli the quieter and cheaper they get. In fact, the tourist factor drops off rapidly – one visit, Lili and I had walked along the Arno for a few blocks and then crossed the river through some side streets, when we came upon an untouristed piazza called Santo Spirito after the medieval church there (if *medieval* and *church* aren't redundant here). We had a cappuccino in an outdoor café under the shade of some pleasant trees and watched the locals, seemingly worlds away from the crowds down the street.

The memorable restaurants and cafés in Florence were all outside of the center, well off the beaten track. One was even off the unbeaten track: we drove for an hour, on dirt roads, until we got there to enjoy fresh game and home-made pasta. Now, maybe there was a major road on the other side, but you learn never to tell an Italian how to drive.

Lucca

The first thing I noticed about Lucca was the terrible driving. I had been driving in Italy for over eight months by the time we came here and I had never before seen such reckless driving as here. The roads around the historic center are in a ring, and the drivers here think they are on a circular race track. But it wasn't just the speed: it was speed in very bad areas, like curves and corners that bothered me. I'm not a slow driver, but I was cut off on exits and turns more than once or twice by drivers entirely too eager to beat me to the next red light. I've been told that the drivers in the South are worse than the North, which was a really scary thought, looking at the traffic here.

My suspicions were confirmed when we finally breached the city walls. Even getting that far was harrowing: I was standing four feet back from the curb to cross the street and I was still nervous, watching the cars racing at breakneck speeds around narrow curves and passing when there was no room to pass. Once inside, we encountered even more reckless drivers, taking the narrow, pedestrian- and bike-filled winding streets far too fast. The center is not a large area, and would be best served with no cars inside it at all. The fact that there are no sidewalks on the medieval alleys and that the place is very popular with tourists makes for a bad mix, and Lili managed to get hit by an uncaring driver who just had to get a few blocks in a hurry. She wasn't badly hurt but we realized this must happen every day.

My theory is that the poor driving in Italy is directly related to their relaxed attitude about time: there is little regard for punctuality; meaning Italians are usually running late. Every meeting starts late and ends later. The only time they can make up a little time is in their cars, so they drive too fast to get to the next appointment less late but of course that appointment runs late as well, and they are late getting to the next one, and so on.

Back to Lucca. Many people love Lucca for its preserved medieval aspect, including almost complete city walls, now covered with grass and trees.

Lucca was a Roman town, and this explains the regular grid of streets in the central area. Walking in from the San Donato entrance, we came to a church that we took for the duomo. The façade looked like a wedding cake, all white and frilly. Upon inspection I noticed that this was in fact San Michele in Foro, a large Romanesque church built on the old Roman forum (which explains the name). Due to the church's placement over a large part of the square, the market is held elsewhere. The two things I noticed about this church were the light streaming in through the West windows, and the statue hidden in the corner that had been taken off the façade for safekeeping.

Walking down Via Fillungo, Lucca's main street and main shopping street, we passed the clock tower, one of the several towers you can ascend to see the other towers in Lucca. I found it almost useless as a clock tower, since we couldn't see the clock from anywhere in town, the streets are so narrow and the buildings so tall. Nonetheless, it is a major attraction and we stopped and looked up at it, wondering if we looked as silly as everyone else.

Some way further on there is a small, irregular shaped piazza off the right side of the street, with an arched doorway in a curved building. Through it, we could see a large, oval piazza with typical porticoed ochre and yellow buildings on the other side. It was the former site of the Roman amphitheater which had been converted into apartments in medieval times, and was now inhabited by souvenir shops and a few cafés. We made a circuit of the piazza and found an artist who specialized in paintings of the square: most of his paintings were vertical tableaux, showing different lives on each floor of the narrow buildings around the piazza. One showed the life of Pinocchio with a different chapter in each window. We took two and he signed them for us. It wasn't until we left the amphitheatre by another door that I realized the houses we saw were built inside the Roman amphitheater walls, which can still be seen on the outside of some of the houses. So all was not lost of the original structure, although most of the stones are now in church and palazzo walls.

One of the best experiences we had in Lucca came while we were taking a street with no tourist attractions on it. The street was called *Via del Angelo Custode*, or Guardian Angel Street. The houses here were tall and reworked several times, as evidenced by the mismatched brick and the filled-in window frames. As we walked, we heard someone singing opera, accompanied on the piano. We stopped under the window and listened for a while. From this street we could also glance into the windows of a few apartments, where we could see a moment of people's everyday lives. We saw the arched ceilings and dark furniture that characterize most of the houses we have seen in Italy.

A few archways and a piazza later, we came to the duomo. The bell tower had been built before the present-day church, so the façade was cut off on one side. The details here are most impressive: each column was carved by a different artisan, so they are all different. There are also impressive statues by Pisano and della Quercia in the loggia. There is a strange ornate, round cage inside the duomo, called the *Tempietto* (little temple). Inside is a carved wood *Deposition*, purported to have been carved by Nicodemus at the time of the actual event but upon inspection (through the bars, at a distance, in poor light) it looked medieval to me. There is also a Tintoretto painting in the aisle here, and it gets a lot of attention. Perhaps I have been seeing too much pop art to be impressed by yet another Renaissance artist painting yet another *Last Supper*. Or perhaps I'm just saturated with "high" art, but I was unimpressed.

There is a crypt in the duomo that houses a well-known and quite impressive tomb of Ilaria del Carretto carved by Jacopo della Quercia. We had seen it on several post cards and were eager to see the original until we found that the church had started charging (and quite a lot, at that) to see it. If there had been other artifacts to see, or something very impressive, we might have considered it. As it was, we had seen enough marble statues and enough postcards of this one to skip it.

We stopped briefly in the Church of Saints Giovanni e Reparata, which is best known for the excavations of the Roman temple that was here before a church was built over it. You can't see much besides a fragment of mosaic flooring and then some remnants from the earlier churches on this site. It reminded me of San

Clemente in Rome, with its layers of history excavated beneath the present structure.

This is interesting not only from an architectural standpoint but also from a religious one. Most early churches were built on top of older pagan shrines, as a way of acknowledging the gods of the culture they were supplanting as well as a way to benefit from any power or force that may exist in that spot. As heretical as the idea may sound today, it was a very expedient way to attract more converts to the early Church. You can see the solid evidence in other churches as well: Notre Dame in Paris, and the cathedrals in Chartres and Mexico City.

In the piazza alongside the church we found an empty café and sat down for a cappuccino. The cappuccino here was decent, although nothing special. The most memorable part was the large umbrella that was anchored by a curved steel pole. The thing would have been a trick to anchor in calm weather, but a wind had picked up that brought the café owner and his family out just to keep it from blowing over and taking the better part of the café with it. A British couple that had sat down found it just a little too much for them and left fairly quickly.

From there, we walked a few blocks and came out in a large, tree-lined piazza that reminded me of the best squares in France. Coincidentally, it was named Piazza Napoleone, after Napoleon, who had given Lucca to his sister to rule. Chalk one up for women's liberation! This one was lined with cafés and elegant buildings in pleasing colors. On this particular day the piazza was rather full, due to a concert that evening by an American pop artist. The act had drawn almost every American in Tuscany to Lucca, which also meant there were no hotel rooms available.

By now, Palazzo Pfanner was closed. This was the home of a rich Lucchese family in the 17th century with an impressive, statue-filled garden. Having missed it, we decided to take in a small exhibit in the basement of another 17th century palazzo. It is amazing what can hide behind a simple, innocuous façade and I started to understand the proverb about judging a book by its cover. Behind a discreet wall and gate, we found a huge garden surrounding a small estate. With the overcrowding and tall apartment buildings in most of the town, we wondered how someone had found the room to build this. The exhibit showed some of the Roman and medieval ruins found in Lucca during road works and basement reconstructions. The most striking displays were mosaic floors, complicated wall decorations and vanity items: fine ivory hair picks, wine glasses, and jewelry.

The hour was getting late, and we had seen just about all Lucca had to offer, the rest being minor churches and the city walls. Due to the concert that night we did not have a hotel room so we had two choices: forge on to Pisa and look for a hotel there, or head home and try again some other day. The drive home was short, so we chose the latter.

Out Of Italy

Lugano

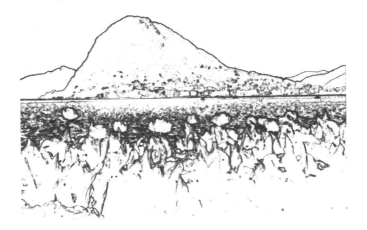

I might have said this before, but I am in love with Switzerland. The mountains, the lakes, the green, the roads, the banks – it all adds up to something close to perfection. Lugano is just half an hour north of Milan, and even though the people here speak Italian, it is most decidedly a foreign country. Lugano is sited logically along the banks of Lake Lugano. The walk along the water is sublime, with the hills rising on all sides, and the curious trees shading the walk. The weather here is subtropical and there are palm trees – in Switzerland! Lugano is warmer and sunnier than Milan, due to the mountains that separate them.

As we first drove into town, I had a few concerns: our car was running on fumes, I didn't have a map, the police were handing out speeding and parking tickets, and today was a national holiday meaning hotel rooms were scarce and pricey. My worries turned out to be baseless, as we found parking, a hotel and gas although not necessarily in that order.

Lugano will go down in my memory as a warm and sunny place, while in Italy the weather was cold and gray. It was so warm that we took a boat trip out around the lake and drowsed on warm stone benches in hillside villages overlooking the lake and the green hills surrounding it.

Lucerne

We were on our way to Germany to visit some friends near Heilbronn. We had last seen them in March in Vigo di Fassa in the Dolomites, where we had skied together and we were looking forward to seeing them again. Vigo di Fassa and Cortina d'Ampezzo are amazingly beautiful and fun places to visit and I'm sorry I didn't write about them this time. We had decided to drive, since the weather was fine and we wanted to make some stops along the way. The quickest way to southwest Germany from Italy is through Switzerland (the alternative was through Austria), via Lugano, Lucerne and Zurich.

Since our earlier trip to Lugano, I had decided that Switzerland had some monopoly on beauty. Our drive north, through summer weather, with waterfalls dotting the rock cliffs and the highest mountain peaks still covered in snow above, reinforced my conclusion. Everything about Switzerland seems perfect, cared for, especially in contrast to Italy. Even the roadsides, for example: in Italy, the shoulder is mostly a collection of dirt and cigarette butts. In Switzerland, there is well-tended grass with no trash in sight. The hills are beautiful collections of fields, houses or trees, and the villages that lead down to the lakeshores around the improbably blue Lake Lucerne look like they were made to be photographed.

We didn't spend much time here, but made a mental note to return to this scion of beauty.

Heilbronn

Well, Germany isn't really known for its coffee, so we just had beer. Good beer, though, fresh and cheaper than water. This region is also full of vineyards and the locals are proud of their wine production even though the wine is not very good.

Heilbronn was a pleasant enough place, with a large pedestrian zone and plenty of bars. There is also an island, very green, with its own beer garden and a hotel almost surrounded by the river. We were drinking here with a group of Germans – friends of friends – when the sky opened up and rain came down in buckets. We ran to a table with a large canvas umbrella, which was closed at the time since it was broken. Well, we rigged it as best we could, and huddled under it with our liters of beer. Gradually we finished them and the rain also died down. By then it was getting dark and we had only had pretzels and bratwurst to eat, so we took the opportunity to leave. We stopped in a small town on the way home and picked up some Thai food which was a welcome relief to the nonstop Italian food we had been eating.

Angers

I like Angers (pronounced Ahn-*zhay*). It is a simple city, unpretentious, friendly and approachable but still cosmopolitan. The traditional stone buildings all around were warm and handsome in the sun. Winter may be cold and sad, with cobblestone streets running up hills by large stone walls, but in the summer it was light and inviting and very green. Angers is the home of the Plantagenets, who became the royal family of France and of England. The city has a feeling of previous glory and the huge fortified castle in the center of town, started in the Ninth century, is a constant reminder of that past. There seems to be a feeling here of pride in that past, although it never seemed to become overwhelming.

What I liked best about Angers are its brasseries, one next to the other lining every major street. They are all equally inviting — some are sophisticated, others traditional or modern, but all have a charm. The coffee here comes in a small cup and is not as strong as elsewhere in France. Wherever we went, coffee and a crepe were the perfect combination and we were never once disappointed. Perhaps the best one we tried was called Le Petit Comptoir. It is far from the Place du Ralliement, and fills with locals for lunch. Somehow they have squeezed a second level of dining area above the bar. Le Petit Comptoir serves a special dish which comes highly recommended: toasted dark bread topped with various combinations (*tapenade* with anchovies, *fromage blanc aux herbes*, et cetera).

Angers is a quick trip from Paris by TGV (high speed train) but is off the tourist trail meaning you get more value for your money: food and hotels are roughly half the price of Paris, for example. It is in striking distance of the Loire Valley, however, with the latter's offering of chateaux.

Tours

Tours is one of the stops that I would recommend to anyone interested in seeing a part of France generally off the main tourist maps. Don't get me wrong, there were plenty of tourists here, but the town was not packed with them like Paris gets in summer. Like Angers, it is also a good base for discovering the Chateaux along the Loire.

Tours is a mid-sized town with an old center of pedestrian streets among half-timbered houses. It is more than pleasant, but having come from Angers, the difference for me was Tours's broad avenues with wide islands and huge sidewalks lined with tree-shaded cafes. The streets were busy with locals, doing errands, shopping, and relaxing at the numerous cafes.

Moulins

We stopped in Moulins because I liked the name (which means Windmills). It also broke up a drive from northwest France to the southeast. Other than that, there's not much to recommend it.

There may well have been windmills here when they named the place, but they are long gone now. There's not much else to see, either: the center is a very small place, not particularly pretty or historic. There is an old tower: La Malcoiffée (the messy-headed). Not much to look at, and, as the nearby explanation says, even the Renaissance didn't leave much of an impact here.

The town looked deserted when we got there. Adding to the desolation was the weather that day, cold and rainy – not exactly summer weather!

We walked around and realized that everyone who was still in town was eating lunch: the restaurants and cafes were full. We stopped at the main café in town, Les 3 Ducs, and stood at the counter. The coffee there was hot and strong, but not the best I've tasted – a little disappointing, especially for the price. Lili had a good hot chocolate, and it hit the spot for this wintry July day. The proprietor, it turns out, had worked in Mexico years ago, speaks several languages, and enjoys meeting foreigners. We took a few more pictures and left Moulins in the rain.

Lyons

On the way, I thought about Lyons. I knew it was a big city (second or third largest in France), known for its food and I expected to like it. After a bit of confusion on the road in (look for the signs to Presqu'Ile, which is the center), we made it to Vieux Lyon, the old town.

I disagree with those who say Lyons is ugly and with those who say it's pleasant. It was a mix of both. The old town (perhaps not surprisingly) was packed with tourists and those making money off of them. There were so many tourists and distractions, in fact, that we could not walk down the narrow street. We noticed that you could walk on a side street unmolested, while seeing the same old buildings and cafés. Once we found these side streets, the old town became almost pleasant, but not so impressive as to keep us there.

We decided that the town was too full of tourists and the hotels seemed full, so we left without stopping for coffee. I am pleased to say that the road out was easier than the road in, although finding the road to Grenoble was next to impossible.

Grenoble

Grenoble is a very pleasant place, with a center filled with people and shops. The pedestrian zones extend much longer than they do in other cities, and somehow there are shops to fill them all. The night we arrived, starving, we were thrilled to find two entire blocks of kebab shops, Lebanese and Turkish restaurants. For about €5 each, we had shish kebab, drinks and fries.

The streets and cafes were particularly full that Sunday night because it was Bastille Day and everyone was out for the fireworks that were to start at 10:30, a little after full darkness had fallen. The fireworks were great. Everyone gathered on the river's edge where the roads were closed to traffic.

On the drive down, we were afraid of spending the night in some small town where the celebrations would be minimal or disappointing. But we had managed to get to Grenoble, where the fireworks were spectacular, launched from the Bastille fortress over the river. The spectacle lasted about half an hour, and I felt that I had never been so close to a fireworks display.

The next day, realizing there wasn't much to do in Grenoble, we went to the movies. We thought about seeing the cathedral and the crypt, the recently uncovered remains of a 5th century baptistery, but after nine months in Italy and this trip through France, we are churched out and my allergy to museums is stronger than ever. Our conscience got the better of us though and after two days we did venture into the cathedral. We poked around for almost five minutes before we had seen enough – it's not a very impressive place, after all.

We did, however, find some good coffee. There is no lack of cafes here, some with more personality than others. The one across from the cathedral, Tonneau, looks like a cave, with its rounded ceilings. It has a bookstore upstairs, adding almost too much sophistication but if you sit outside you can enjoy your coffee without noticing. The coffee here is strong, and comes in a generous cup. John's Café probably has the friendliest service in town, if not the best *pain au chocolat*. You can bring your own bread, however, so try that.

We left Grenoble a few days later for Briançon, in the Alps, where we were meeting some friends. The road (N91) was beautiful, despite the weather.

Back Again

Ventimiglia

When is a city not a city? When it's a border town and all conventional ideas of good and clean seem to vanish along dark, dirty alleyways with unwelcoming names. My first impression when someone speaks the word Ventimiglia is *seedy*. The city seems to have no center, just street after street of similar buildings with crumbling, nondescript facades, streets that lead only back to the main road out. There is a beach here, but there is hardly enough wet sand to make it worthy of the name. It's hard to believe that only an imaginary boundary and a few miles separate it from the glamorous beaches of the French Riviera. In much the same way, the cardboard hovels of Tijuana seem to be worlds away from the gleaming skyline of San Diego. Like anywhere, there are some things to see and do here. Topping the list of reasons to be here is the market, which is every Friday. Many French people come across the border to buy liquor, knock-off designer clothes and (of course) Italian food. We didn't stop for cappuccino, not this time although a year later I would be back to meet the new owners of a well-known radio station and we ate a decent pasta downstairs from the (rather scary and dark) office.

Siena

Let me begin with the end: we left Siena late in the evening, having seen a great deal and believing that there was a lot we had not seen. Despite the crowds and the heat, there was more to see than Lucca, yet more accessible than Florence and more colorful than other medieval hill towns.

It surprised me that we had never been to Siena before, since we had been in Florence at least 10 times over the year. There is a free road (*superstrada*) from there, which makes it less of a trek than Pisa or Bologna but somehow we just hadn't taken it. Finally, we just had to force it onto our schedule. Of course, we didn't take the superstrada all the way, since we had started out south of Florence in Reggello. We took a local road that looked more or less direct on the map, which turned out to be the world's windiest road, so we were a bit behind schedule for lunch in town.

We stopped for lunch somewhere on the road near Castellina in Chianti, at a roadside restaurant with patio seating. It was a pretty location on a hill, overlooking the Tuscan countryside which is easily among the loveliest in the world. The old painted sign read *Bar Ristorante*, and I never learned the name of the place. It was ready for tourists, though: the waitresses spoke no Italian, just English and German (which is all you hear in Tuscany in the summer, anyway). We had arrived at 1:30 – half an hour after lunchtime, so we were lucky to be served. Over the next 45 minutes, we watched, trying not to smirk, as no less than four other couples parked and sat down for a late lunch, only to be turned away because the restaurant was closed. We had been caught once too often in the same situation and had become resigned to the intransigent Italian eating schedule without ever liking it. Now we fairly bolted for the nearest trattoria if we hadn't eaten by 1:45 and weren't on or near the Autostrada.

We arrived in Siena in early afternoon, after the worst of the heat had gone but with plenty of light left in the day. We were tempted to park outside the walls, but the hill dropped rapidly, meaning a long walk up in the heat and the closest space was quite a distance down. So we bit the bullet and parked in a garage just inside the walls.

Siena, we read, is divided into *contrade*, or districts, each one represented by an animal. We were expecting the usual: lions, tigers, eagles, etc. (and those are here) but were happily surprised to see that the *contrada* where we were parked was...the snail. The second one we walked through on our way to the main square, the Piazza del Campo, was the turtle. You see these animals represented in fountains, on wrought-iron announcement boards and on building façades as well as the omnipresent Sienese flags, made famous by the Palio, a twice-annual horse race around the Piazza del Campo supposedly since at least 1283.

Every guide book worth the name gives a description of the Palio, so I will content myself with just the bare essentials. Feel free to consult Lonely Planet or Dorling Kindersley for more information. The Palio is run on July 2 and August 16. Like the residents of Monte Carlo during the Grand Prix there, the sensible Sienese leave town during that time. And I concur: although I dearly love horses and enjoy a good horse race as well as the colorful medieval pageantry. The thought of being packed liked a sardine into the center of the piazza with 100,000 of my closest friends under the summer sun with only a glimpse of flying flags or dashing horses didn't sound like fun. Instead, we watched it on TV from the safety and comfort of our apartment – the view was better, and we could reminisce about what we saw in Siena. Also, the souvenirs are available year round.

At any rate, we finally made it to the Piazza del Campo. It is quite a large square, shaped like a fan (on purpose) that gently slopes up towards the curved edges which are lined with cafés, restaurants and souvenir shops. The Palazzo Pubblico, the immense red brick castle with its 335-foot bell tower, faces the curve of the shops around the fan. It was too severe for my taste, and the bell tower impossibly high for a medieval city, but that didn't stop anyone from enjoying the square. The palazzo is a museum inside, and houses some well-known paintings and frescoes, including the *Allegory of Good and Bad Government* by Lorenzetti and another of *Guidoriccio da Fogliano*, the familiar scene of a knight in red and gold harlequins riding a horse dressed the same. This being a museum, we didn't stay long.

The streets around the piazza are very pleasant. This place is certainly made for tourists, and the tourists were certainly there. Despite the crowds, the streets were not unpleasant and the few shopkeepers we encountered were friendly and hospitable. The streetlamps in the central area were very unusual, shaped like trees with several small bulbs. Wandering around, we found a fair number of very old shops selling medicine, wine, and odds and ends in gothic stone buildings. Since the streets in Sienna are neither straight Roman roads nor concentric rings around the central piazza, we were lost in a very short time. We found what must have been the only empty street in Siena: an alley covered by brick arches with completely covered alleys leading out. Once again, we were struck with the thought that medieval times were dark in more ways than one.

We finally found our way out to a street with a view of San Domenico – not a pretty church, but large and imposing. We never made it to the inside, which was a shame since the head of St. Catherine, Siena's patron saint, is on display here.

It was almost time for a coffee when we reached the duomo but we almost forgot that, we were so impressed. We followed the signs here, and still managed to approach from an unexpected angle. The problem isn't so much that the signs are wrong, it's just that there are always at least two ways to get anywhere and there are frequently signs at an intersection pointing both left and right with the same destination on them. The locals already know which way to go, it's only confusing for tourists but maybe that's the point. What's more, they keep offering choices until you are almost at the destination. I reckon we added more than a few extra kilometers to our trip this way.

We made our way up the steps from the baptistery to the piazza that runs alongside the duomo. The first thing we noticed was that the church (like the duomo in Bologna) is unfinished. Here, however, you have an indication of the size of the plans: over 150 feet away from the present walls, you see an immense inner façade of matching marble and realize you are standing in what would have been the nave and the current church would have been the transept. The church here is unfinished due to a death in the family: over half of Siena's population died in the Plague of 1348 and the rest didn't need a larger church after that.

The Duomo is black and white striped marble and large. It is considered among the finest of Italy's churches, and I am inclined to agree. From the beautiful façade, with its intricate statues and carvings to the inlaid marble floor, with portraits, designs and allegories, to the incredibly carved pulpit by Pisano (too bad you have to stand so far away) and the statues of popes by Michelangelo and, finally, to the chapel of St John the Baptist, in which there is a statue by Donatello. This was perhaps the highlight for me. Whereas Michelangelo's works are all finely done and of masterful quality, Donatello's seem to embody a modern sensibility: his

John the Baptist here is no hero; he is tired, his clothes in rags. In Florence, his *David* is the opposite of Michelangelo's hero: where Michelangelo's is an oversized portrait of triumph and energy, Donatello's is young and almost effeminate. I stood a while to admire the statue. The small chapel, with the unmarked statue, was practically empty the entire time.

We also paused to admire the exposed portion of the *Slaughter of the Innocents* on the floor. The entire floor is exquisitely decorated with inlaid marble art and portraits here, but only small portions are on display while the rest is covered with cardboard. A fair part of the *Slaughter* was exposed while we were there as well as some portraits in the southern aisle and we were simply blown away. It would be great if the floor could be covered with, say, Plexiglas and thus entirely visible. But this is

Italy, and if cardboard and masking tape have been good enough for the last hundred years, then it's good enough to cover the floor for the next hundred. Apparently the floor is uncovered for a few weeks in August or September, you guess which weeks.

In the north aisle, there is a small doorway (look for the ticket booth) leading to the Piccolomini library, a small museum built into the church by the Piccolomini family. The Piccolominis (*piccolo* means small in Italian, so one wonders about the size of the family members) ironically were a prominent family in Siena, whose influence increased when one of the sons became a pope (Pius II) – his portrait is one of the many frescoes covering the walls in the library. Some of the largest books (OK, *the* largest books) I've ever seen are open on display here: the pages are at least four feet high which must have made them easy to read from a distance or were written for someone with very bad eyes. While coming out of the library, we looked up and noticed busts of hundreds of popes along both sides of the nave, halfway to the ceiling. Some of them are downright scary, glaring down with disapproving looks at the faithful. Farther up, the ceiling was painted a dark blue with gold stars.

From the "Only in Italy" department comes the small figure of Mary in an alcove in the southern transept. The statue is unremarkable except that she performs miracles and people have left all sorts of items to thank her. Hanging prominently on the wall near the statue are several motorcycle helmets — in case I haven't mentioned it, we have seen dozens of near-death experiences involving scooter and motorcycle riders. The miracle is that so many of them survive as long as they do. Some of the survivors of the daily accidents have given their helmets in tribute to the statue for saving their lives. They would like to come pray in person but they are busy overtaking cars on their repaired bikes, passing them on the wrong side of the road around blind curves.

We almost didn't want to leave the duomo, but we realized that there were other sites to see and we had covered merely a fraction of the town.

The first thing we did on leaving the duomo was start looking for a good café. The closest one was behind the baptistery but it didn't look inviting and was obviously set up just for tourists. Winding our way down some side streets and sidestepping the Piazza del Campo, we came to Piazza Independenza. Being a few blocks from the main square and in the opposite direction from the main sights, it was less crowded and with lower prices than the places on the main drag. We found a small café with two tables out front. We sat down and enjoyed large cups of reasonably priced, mild cappuccino while watching the people pass. We saw many locals walk by, which was a good sign. We could tell them by the briefcases and cellphones, the men wearing blue or yellow cotton suits, the women wearing impossibly high heels on the cobbled pavement, dressed in the latest cheap clothing fashions, the older women looking disapprovingly at the see-through, clingy skirts and frilly tops.

Perugia

Perugia stank – literally. But I'm jumping ahead here. Perugia has a reputation as a very pretty, medieval hill town where the well-known Perugino chocolate comes from. It was highly rated by guidebooks and people who had been there so it was a must-see on our list.

Coming from Siena, we were looking forward to another jewel. So at first I disregarded the traffic, which was rivaled only by Lucca's, for blatant rudeness and dangerous practices. Sitting in line for 20 minutes just to drive into the parking garage, however, the drivers began to wear on my patience. By the time we were parked and had gotten up to the old town, we were starved and I was in a pretty sour mood. Adding insult to injury, we waited 30 minutes after finally ordering food that never came before we simply walked away from one of the many restaurants on the Corso Vanucci. We ended up eating sandwiches that we made ourselves from cheese and deli meat from a *Coop* grocery, miraculously placed on Via Baglioni, which runs parallel to Corso Vanucci. I highly recommend Coop delis for a delicious lunch. Bring your own knife.

Then it began to rain. I wish this weren't true but there we were, eating these huge sandwiches on the steps on the side of the duomo (I'm not sure why there were steps on the side, but at the time I didn't really question it), staring at Perugia's main fountain (newly restored) with the town's main building, the Palazzo dei Priori, behind it. The clouds came extremely quickly from the opposite direction of the wind, and we knew there would be trouble. At the first sign of rain, we scrambled for cover under a portico, conveniently located right next to the steps we were on. About one minute later, half the tourists in Perugia were there with us, speaking a babble of languages. We finished our sandwiches and ran for the Palazzo dei Priori during a lull. Since it was still lunchtime, the parts of the building we wanted to see were closed. During the next lull in the rain, we made a break for the garage and left town.

In addition to the handy portico alongside the duomo, I also enjoyed the underground entrance to the public escalators that lead down to the smelly area around the bus station and garages. Once inside the unmarked door for the escalators, we looked up and realized we were in an exceedingly high basement, with huge brick arches and winding tunnels (most of them well-lit) heading off all around us. They were empty, but fascinating – and hardly worth the trip by themselves.

Assisi

In striking contrast to Perugia, Assisi was a highlight of our short trip. We almost didn't make it. Discouraged by Perugia and faced with a lightning storm to the east, Assisi wasn't looking very promising. We continued to drive towards the storm, which had completely blackened the entire sky east of us, wondering if the storm would be over Assisi. We were under the black cloud, when we hit the exit and had to decide.

We looked up on the hill, and saw Assisi, stone spires and walls, halfway up the hill. It was in the sun, the clouds and rain hitting just the eastern edge of the town. Lightning was all over the horizon, though, and a change in the wind would soak it. We'd come this far though, so we figured we may as well have a look. Getting to Assisi is easy: follow the stream of cars and buses uphill until you come to a parking area that you like. Having been in places like this before, I knew to aim as high as possible up the slope. We finally came to one that said *Centro 250m*, so we parked there which was fine, as the walk up went through olive groves outside the city walls.

The same forces that drove us out of Perugia seemed to want us to visit Assisi as the sun shone all afternoon on the city and dried the streets and café tables. The light on the damp buildings sparkled and glowed and made the town even more attractive than the flowers and frescoed walls there.

Most people know Assisi as the home of St. Francis, and his basilica there is certainly impressive. I thoroughly enjoyed the lower church, which was subdued and low-key (relatively speaking, that is: Giotto and Cimabue had covered almost every available surface with frescoes). It was devoid of hanging, protruding and otherwise interfering artefacts, knickknacks or decorations. Fitting, I thought, for someone as humble as St. Francis. The only drawback was a recording of a harsh Italian voice saying, "Silence, please" in five languages.

What most people probably don't see when they come to Assisi is the fantastic medieval hill town where St. Francis actually lived. It's not the shortest hike, but it is well worth the stroll. Walking away from the upper church, we took the Via San Francesco which changes names once or twice but leads all the way through the city. The shops along the way mostly sold souvenirs and artworks, but unlike most towns, the souvenirs here were devoted to St. Francis, meaning there were lots of animals in every shape and size in addition the more common crucifixes and prayer tiles. We noticed that the souvenirs dropped in price as we got further from the basilica until we came close to the main square.

About halfway through the walk we came to a piazzetta, barely more than a fork in the road, where we found a café in the triangular point. It was time for an afternoon caffeine boost anyway, so we stopped and sat down. The owner was polite and efficient and the drinks were large and just right – strong but not bitter, hot but not scalding. The view was limited to the streets going up and down from the fork, but the houses there were quite agreeable to stare at for a while. When the bill came, we realized that perfection, alas, comes at a price.

Under the main square, the Piazza del Comune, are the ruins of the Roman forum that gave the piazza its current shape. I poked my head in the door but the museum was closing and we preferred to see the top of the piazza, anyway. The main square is dominated by a Roman temple to Minerva (now a church on the inside but the façade is preserved) and a 13th century town hall, now an art gallery. It is not a large square but was comfortable in size, and the buildings rising onto the hill above and the quaint steps going down to the streets below made it very pleasant. Even with the large number of tourists and pilgrims there, the place was quiet and uncrowded.

Walking out of the piazza, we came to the Basilica di Santa Chiara, a disciple of Francis, who began Poor Clares, an order of nuns. By the time we got there the basilica was closed, which was a shame. There didn't seem to be too much inside but it was a handsome church, and I had read that the cross that had spoken to St. Francis was here. Why it should be in Clare's, and not Francis' basilica is a mystery to me, but then the cross came from another church altogether and should probably still be there and not propped in a basilica at all.

Since we couldn't get in, we wandered around the piazza in front of the church which was a very lucky thing: the view from the piazza was stunning. The sun was beginning to go down, and the light all around was gold, making the stone buildings all around literally glow against the sky. The black sky behind us emphasized the profile of the town, highlighting the olive-covered hills below the town, then the walls, towers and the taller buildings in it.

Down below us, the green valley, with Santa Maria degli Angeli and its large domed church in the foreground looked like a painting. A photograph would not have done justice to the light and colors, which was just as well since we had forgotten the camera in the car, a 15-minute hike down the hill. Instead, we stood and engraved the image into our minds: Assisi, golden in the sunset, the bad weather behind us.

It was truly a superlative moment and we toyed with the idea of staying here – there are inexpensive hotels, and we would be happy to stroll around such a beautiful place for another day. But brevity being the soul of beauty (or something like that) – and, more to the point, being out of clean underwear – we decided to head home.

Cremona

It was towards the end of August and Italy was still closed. It was a very pleasant time to be around: no crowds, no traffic. The downside was that life was suspended: no movies open in Italy during August, and there are no concerts or events or fairs. In addition, many restaurants close, narrowing the selection available. Still, for those who know where to go, this is only a minor annoyance.

To take advantage of the quiet, we decided to visit a place we had never been, and chose Cremona for its proximity and attractions. Cremona is not a large, busy or very touristy place, and there are not a hundred monuments to run around and see. For that reason, it was a very quiet and pleasant place to spend a day.

Anyone who has heard of Cremona knows it for one thing: its violins. Amati invented the violin here and Stradivarius, a native, perfected the art. His workshop can still be visited (for a fee). Walking around the city we saw reminders of this heritage in every shop window: you can buy violin key chains, violin liquor bottles, violin paintings, violin postcards, violin tie clips and violin necklaces. It's a wonder the kids don't turn to violin crime (heh, heh).

Cremona is not far from Milan and is also well connected to Mantova and Pisa. Piacenza, another unvisited but pleasant town on the Via Emilia, is about 20km from Cremona, although Piacenza is part of Emilia-Romagna and Cremona is in Lombardy. The drive in was uneventful, which was fine with me. It was 1:45

when we could see the downtown area, and it was evident we were not going to make it to town, park and find a restaurant before 2:00. Danger! Danger!

I saw a trattoria on the side of the road and we pulled over and dashed in, just making it before the chef called it a day (the next guy was turned away). We were lucky: what I had seen was no more than a doorway in a large, sun-baked wall and a sign above it. Inside, it was dark and cool. We walked out back into a courtyard that Lili found very pleasant and I found dizzying: the floor was tilted to allow rain to run off, but the pattern in the concrete was concentric circles intersected by radiating lines. I could have avoided looking down, but then the walls were covered in very thin bamboo, which clashed painfully with the circular pattern on the floor. Lili had a view of flowerpots lining the low wall that gave onto the courtyard.

Luckily, service was prompt and the food was good. There was no written menu, so the waitress (who bore an uncanny resemblance to her mother and grandmother who were also working there) told us what was on today — always a strange experience for us, but then most Italians already know what they want when they walk in, so they don't need a written menu.

I had the *gnocchi al pesto*. Pesto is almost nonexistent in Emilia-Romagna (it's not a local specialty so you just don't see it), and I missed it. The gnocchi were home made, another nice touch. We thought about having coffee, but decided to take it in the center instead. That was fine with the owners, they had already closed the metal barrier over the front door and were ready to go upstairs and rest. In spite of that, they were very friendly and didn't rush us. The entire meal, including the *coperto*, came to less than €10.

When we arrived in the center around 3:00, it was still sleeping. We walked through the deserted streets until we reached the main square, Piazza del Comune. We had come from the south, so we actually passed through the courtyard of the Palazzo Comunale (town hall) to get here. There was nothing special about the building, it was just another medieval brick palazzo with arched, frescoed ceilings and a portico giving onto the piazza. In the wall on one side was a café, its tables in the arches and out onto the square, most of the shady tables taken by old men with newspapers.

Walking out into the cobbled piazza, we admired the buildings all around: the palazzo comunale had pointed crenellations running along the top. Across a small street was a smaller, matching building with an open ground floor, now a war memorial. Facing the palazzo was the duomo, an impressive Pisan-looking façade with an arched portico that ran the length of the square to link the church to the bell tower. The bell tower, called *Il Torrazzo*, is claimed to be the tallest medieval tower in Italy, the tallest brick tower in Europe, or the tallest bell tower attached to a Romanesque church. In other words, it's tall but a qualified tall.

Compared to the town around it, the tower is immense. There is a clock on the front that shows the hour, the month, the zodiac sign, and other things that were important to the medieval people looking at it. To give some indication of the size, the clock is practically legible from the city walls and it is near the base of the tower. The view from the top allowed the town ample time to prepare for any oncoming attacks (being built on the Po Plain, Cremona needed all the warning it could get because it was otherwise pretty indefensible).

On the other side of the church, forming a third wall of the piazza, is the baptistery. Like the ones in Parma and Pisa, this building is tall and octagonal. Two of the sides, the façade and the side closest to the church, were covered with the same marble as the church façade. Otherwise it was brick. Unlike Pisa or Parma, there was nothing inside the baptistery except for brick walls and two ungainly Baroque statues at opposite ends.

We had just enough time to examine these buildings when a small door to the duomo was opened by an old priest who then made his way back inside. The entire contingent of tourists in Cremona (about a dozen of us) made our way in. The interior was impressive: not a square inch of wall or ceiling had been left unfrescoed. The ceiling and most of the walls had been decorated during the Renaissance (the current façade dated from the same period). The old

Gothic arches had also been squared off to become more classical. The transepts looked a little more original with their vaulted ceilings covered by medieval frescoes with simple colors and naïve designs. The altars (all three) were quite baroque and impressive but overall not really noteworthy. In a wall incongruously placed between the side altars and the main one were steps down to the crypt. Even this wall was frescoed, painted to look like a house with a shelter over the door and windows above.

The crypt contains what might be euphemistically referred to as the body of Saint Omobono, the first layperson to be canonized. Omobono apparently fought against heresy in his day. He is on display in an elegant glass casket. He is dressed in an elegant period costume, a velvet robe, gloves and embroidered moccasins. The head is evidently elsewhere, and instead there is a silver sculpture of a dead Omobono, his eyes closed. The shoes are simply propped up where the feet should be and I wondered where they might be now. There was so little of him left, in fact, that I wondered if it could even be correctly called the body of a saint.

The north wall of the crypt contained the bone of yet another saint, a San Antonio (not *the* San Antonio, whose whole body is in Padova). There was an elaborate tomb in an alcove to him, and an altar in front of it. Above the altar was a glass-sided reliquary. It was dark in the crypt, and even darker in the alcove, and darker still under the tomb but there was no mistaking the good sized bone, broken at one end and darkened with age and dirt, inside the glass box. It really didn't look so much like a saint's bone, as something that the dog might have dug up.

Judging from the color of the bone, it was just possible that the priest's dog had, in fact, found this. The story would have gone like this: A few hundred years ago, when the Church ruled all aspects of European life, a priest in Cremona had gotten home from walking his dog. Since it was the cook's day off, he had stopped and picked up some Chinese takeout on the way home. The dog had been running around the poor areas of town and had picked up a nice bone, probably a sheep or a cow that had been slaughtered for dinner. The dog continued to play with the bone while the priest ate, breaking off a sizeable piece that he would not part with. After dinner, the priest would have tried to pull the used thing away from the dog, to throw it away, but his dog would not part with the half he was still working on. The priest was able to grab the other piece, though, which he would have placed in one of the empty takeout boxes.

That evening the priest might have had a visit from a churchwoman who had come by to sweep his quarters, which she did once a month. The devout but simple woman, hungry for faith, may have mistaken the box for a medieval reliquary containing a saintly artifact. The woman would have taken the box directly to the church, figuring the priest was on his way to do just that himself, and she would save him the trip. The priest would have figured that the woman had taken the trash out for him and it would not have been until a week or so later, when the deacon addressed the priests regarding a special ceremony later that month in which they would put this saint's bone which had miraculously appeared just the week before, on public display. To say anything at this point would not be simply embarrassing; since the deacon had accepted the thing as a piece of Saint Anthony, it would be heresy. The best the priest could do now was to hold his tongue and keep his dog away from the crypt.

Aside from the two saints, there were a fair number of marble slabs on the floor, marking the resting places of some of Cremona's leading citizens 500 years ago. These were mostly worn out but some inscriptions were still legible. A few of the figures were of knights in armor. These figures are curiosities now, but I wouldn't have wanted to be around at the time: The normal stench of unwashed people (the Church forbade bathing as sinful) and unwashed clothing, not to mention the animals that were brought into the church on market days, must have been a powerful mix. Add to that the stench of decomposing bodies under your feet every Sunday.

I went back upstairs to the main church, brushing the willies off my arm. In the north transept was a large crucifix that used to adorn the altar here. It is a solid silver construction from the 14th century, carved with over 100 saints (including Cremona's own St. Omobono of course) holy figures, and symbols, including an albatross (an early Christian symbol, since the albatross feeds its young with its own blood if it can't find food for them).

Also on display is a smaller version of the clock on the bell tower. This one, for all its being indoors, is in considerably worse shape than its external counterpart: the paint is cracking and flaking. The hands don't look like they've moved in centuries (this is plausible). The way it is mounted, in a dark corner of a wall partly covered by a trompe l'œil mural, it doesn't look to be the highlight of the church the way the astronomical clock in St. Jacques in Lyons, which is a star attraction.

We left the church through the north transept and were rewarded with a row of cafés and shops along that small road. We were ready to stop and try a cap but decided to explore just a bit more, first. We took the first promising road, Via Solferino, a small cobblestone pedestrian street that ran to Piazza Roma, with a green park and a fountain. This was not your between-buildings piazza: rather, it was full of rows of tree-shaded benches, all occupied by Cremona's older generation. The park itself, all trees and lawns, was separated from the sitting area by a marble balustrade and stairs.

We walked around the square and staring back at the old ladies who stared at us. It wasn't a mean stare, just the typical Italian way of looking at someone. During our time here, we've noticed that the Italians lack what we in the US refer to as manners. It's not that they have *bad* manners, they just don't have *our* manners. Some people say this is due to a peasant background, which continued until well after WWII. Or maybe it's just not the English or American manners. There is a joke, though, about that: An American, a Russian and an Italian are in a grocery store in Rome when they see a sign that reads, "We're sorry, but due to shortages, we have no meat today." The American reads it and says, "What is a shortage?" The Russian reads it and asks, "What is meat?" The Italian reads it and says, "What is sorry?"

If you're on vacation, maybe you can deal with no manners for a week or two without it grating on you. Living with people who bump into you on the sidewalk because they don't feel like moving to one side is another story, however, and this had become a pet peeve of mine. I should note that some American friends of ours live in Milan and the husband is enamored of Italian cuisine (although he cooks at home) and thinks I am far too unforgiving when it comes to Italian "eccentricities". Perhaps I am, but then he is a rather large fellow and when he walks down the street people generally move out of his way.

From the modern buildings surrounding the park, we realized that we were no longer in the historic center of town. Cremona, even a few blocks out from the Piazza del Comune, has quite a lot of modern architecture, generally styled to look like a reenactment of a medieval square. While not as offensive to the eye as some buildings we've seen (particularly in Milan), these were still enough to make us turn and walk the other way to more pleasant streets.

We passed back into Via Solferino, where we found a very nice-looking café on a corner to another small street. It had two tables out front, then four tables lining a wide entrance, and finally another four inside the main room. The interior was warm and tastefully done with wood and chrome, highlighted with halogen spotlights. The owner was very polite and friendly. We ordered two cappuccinos and sat down. The drinks were large and tasty, with coffee just strong enough and a generous amount of foam. They were also probably the cheapest caps we had yet found, despite the central location and decoration of the place. We looked at the menu: if the coffee was any indication of the quality of the food, it would be a great place to stop for dinner. Like lunch, however, there was no written menu here, although the prices listed were very attractive.

Also on Via Solferino was the best candy shop we had ever seen. The window display looked attractive and we decided to pop in to see more. Walking through the door was like a time warp. The shop must have been redesigned last in 1910. The counters, the cash registers, the marbled glass mirrors on the walls, the wooden display cases...everything was exactly as it had been for decades. Even the old women working there must have frequented the shop when they were young. In addition to candy and *torrone* (nougat, a local specialty) the shop sold traditional Italian liqueurs: bitters, limoncello, and grappa.

While not a small town, the interesting part of Cremona is compact. The concentration of shops falls off fairly quickly outside the streets surrounding the Piazza del Comune. While there are certainly buildings and museums to see farther than that, they are not more than three or four blocks distant. The compact center makes for a pleasant walk, and one in which you are pretty sure you will see everything you came to see. We had done just this, looping around to the east, starting behind the duomo and returning past the ex-Basilica di San Lorenzo and ending up back at the park in Piazza Roma.

The town was pretty much in shadow now, but all the shops were still open. The streets were animated with people walking, shopping, talking, and popping into restaurants for an early dinner. We decided to do the same and found a small outdoor Chinese restaurant around the corner from our café. As nice as that café had been, and as good as the prices sounded, we had already had traditional Italian food and really wanted something different. As a rule, sadly, Chinese food in Italy leaves a lot to be desired...especially compared to what you find in the States. The narrow lane was lined with restaurants, one after the other, and on both sides of Via Solferino. The effect was lively and light. After dinner, we joined the flow of people walking around the Piazza del Comune. The piazza was now full of chairs from three different cafés, and it was alive with kids running, animated dinner or post-dinner conversations, and people strolling by.

It was time for us to go, and we headed back towards the car. Leaving Piazza del Comune by a narrow street between the Palazzo Comunale and the Loggia dei Militi, we followed a string of medieval piazzas, each full of people and bars, past diners and drinkers, until we passed a gelateria a few blocks away and left the crowds behind us.

Reggio Emilia

If you are driving by, it's worth slowing down to glance out the window.

Seriously, there is not much to see here. It's a pleasant enough place for a stroll, but Reggio can't compete with its neighbors, Pisa and Modena. If you have limited time, skip it.

As it was, we drove down the Via Emilia one dead August day and walked around the sleeping town. The historic center is blocked to regular traffic so we parked on a side street and walked down the colonnaded street to the center of town. Along the way were plenty of small stores, all closed but showing that the place must be quite animated when people were here.

We expected to come to a central piazza, or something showing that we had reached the exact center of town – the duomo, for instance – but instead we had to consult a map to find the main square and the other sites of interest. We found a small market, mostly selling clothing and bric-a-brac in a piazza in front of the second church, San Prospero. The façade, with its red marble lions and medieval tower looked impressive. The tower is octagonal with forbidding gray stones, and looks quite old – older in fact than it really is (not that it's brand new by a long shot but it's 16th century, while it looks more like Tenth).

From this piazza we followed through an archway into a long courtyard formed by two parallel buildings, the archway and a covered passage, which leads to the main piazza. The main piazza has an interesting, imposing town hall with a large sundial on the front, and frankly the façade outshines the duomo, which looks like an architectural mistake: the core is Romanesque, but there have been so many additions over the ages, in different materials and styles, that it is hard to see a harmony, or even symmetry. At any rate, the inside was nothing spectacular.

The other attraction on the piazza is a room in the Palazzo Pubblico called the Sala del Tricolore – it was here that the Italian flag was designed (by Napoleon, who took the French flag and changed the blue stripe to green): Reggio's claim to fame.

We strolled south along the narrow lanes and found ourselves in Corso Garibaldi, a large piazza full of trees and benches. This piazza was not as old or fancy as the others, but it was much more pleasant. We found a café in one corner and had a bite. We had beer and water – it was too hot for coffee.

By now, it was late afternoon and the locals who had not left on vacation were coming back into the center to meet and shop. The shops that were open were crowded, and the streets were becoming noisy with groups of friends talking, laughing, calling to each other.

It always amazes me, the way life seems to come out of the woodwork in Italian towns. How a city can go from dead to crowded in 30 minutes flat is a phenomenon that I have never gotten over. One minute you're the only person in the entire piazza, every door closed, the next moment people are coming and going to and from every direction, on foot, on bike, on scooters. Walking at midday through the empty, echoing streets you don't see any lights inside the buildings, all the blinds are shut and the doors are closed tight. There is no sound of TV or babies crying or children playing, no sign of life at all. The town is devoid even of traffic at this time. As Mark Twain pointed out, you could shoot a cannon down the street and not hit a thing. Then, at 3:00 (or 4 in smaller towns and in summer) the streets start to come alive. You never see the doors open, but people appear as though they have been there the whole time. Teens walk in noisy groups, talking on their cellphones and window-shopping. Young parents with strollers come seemingly out of thin air, and old women in black and old men wearing suits and hats materialize in alleyways. Before you know it, colorful shops have sprouted out of nondescript walls and people are spilling out onto the sidewalks in front of bars, drinking an *aperitivo*.

We left the town shortly after it had revived. We walked back down the Via Emilia, the sidewalks now crowded and all the shops full of life. We stopped into a few clothing stores (last days of summer sale) and music shops. Lili had seen a cute skirt in a shop window. We walked inside and she looked around. She couldn't find the skirt so she asked. No, they were sold out, even the one on display was sold but they weren't going to take it down just yet and they weren't going to take the price tag off, either. It wasn't the first time we'd seen that, and the Italians seem to be used to things being sold out or out of order without notice.

We drove slowly back down the Via Emilia to Modena. It was almost evening, and we decided to stop downtown and grab a cappuccino on the Piazza Grande before dinner.

San Gimignano

What do you do when you've been in Florence fifteen times in the past ten months, you've seen every street, every piazza, and every other spot of interest in town? You head out of town, of course. This time we went to San Gimignano. It's only about half an hour towards Siena on one of Italy's two good free roads (the other is from Ferrara to Rimini). The location, in between the two most important cities in Tuscany, and the notoriety of its famous architecture, almost explains the crowds here. We arrived in the evening, an hour before darkness fell although we could see it for a good 20 minutes before we got there due to its hilltop position. Driving through the Tuscan countryside is always an inspiring sight, but somehow the anticipation to arrive kept us from fully enjoying the road.

Now, we had spent so much time in Bologna that we were jaded, and medieval towers didn't impress us as much as they impressed those who had come here on a day trip from Florence. Bologna, though, has just a few towers left, and only two of those are notable – the others blend into the architecture, or are dwarfed by more recent (relatively speaking) constructions. Besides, Bologna is a larger city; San Gimignano is tiny, and its two-dozen or more towers are therefore all the more striking.

On every street and square of this tiny but wealthy town, now turned tourist trap, was evidence of these towers built by wealthy families dating back some 800 years. Most of them had been heightened later, as evidenced by the change of materials (brick instead of stone) and patterns (more careless work came later, while the bases were generally solid, large and neatly fitted stones). In fact, most of the buildings here were at least two floors higher than the original medieval work. Built as it was within the city walls, once the vacant lots within had been filled, the only way to build was up. And that's exactly what they did. The buildings, most of them four floors (except for the towers) dwarfed the streets, except for the main street, which was quite wide. It was also packed. Even at this date, at the end of October, on a Sunday evening, the street was so full of visitors you could barely move if you didn't follow the crowd.

As we passed through the city gates, our friends, who were from Florence, made approving gestures, "Is beautiful, no?" I nodded vigorously and smiled: "Si, bella, bella." I had forgotten that Italians look for approval up front, before the experience. In the parking lot even, and before that, on the road when we first saw the towers from 20 kilometers away, they were raving about the place, and didn't we just love it. I said yes, thinking that I would reserve my judgment for later when I had the chance to see the place and form an opinion. Quite un-Italian, it seems.

Andrea, our host and driver, was impatient to get into town, and didn't heed my warning to park in the pay lot. But there was no way he was going to pay some dumb parking lot attendant: he circled and circled to find a spot on the side of the road, which was unfortunate. I say unfortunate because the police in these places make a large part of their revenues from tourists who park illegally: one way or another, you are going to pay for parking here – and it's cheaper to do it in a lot. It was interesting to notice that all the cars parked along the same street were from Italy; the foreigners all seem to have parked in the right place. In these medieval towns, there simply is no parking available and you must park in a pay lot or face a hike up a long hill on a narrow street with no sidewalk. I had found the secret, which was to drive as far as possible until you could not drive any farther, and then find the last lot and park there. It was the closest to the center and was no more expensive than the lots farther out. Plus, since everyone else parks in the first lot they see, the closest lot to town is usually empty. This is valid any time of year, by the way. Anyway, Andrea got a ticket – on Sunday evening – and we still had to walk a distance to and from town.

By the time we had hiked up the hill with the swarms of other late arrivals, it was starting to get dark, which meant it was coffee time. We ran into some of Andrea's friends there, and they also asked us didn't we think San Gimignano was just beautiful. By this time, we had seen the main street and the two piazzas. Of course it was, I said. They had their 13 year-old daughter with them, so we walked down to a chocolate shop, known for its 30 kinds of drinkable chocolate. Now, that sounds a lot more impressive than it really is: I'll bet you've already had a dozen varieties already: dark chocolate, milk chocolate, bitter chocolate, white chocolate, mint chocolate, mocha, and so on – nothing groundbreaking here. So what could we do but have chocolate? Still, the cup was tall and the chocolate was drinkable and almost made up for the brusque service.

Along the street on the way out, we stopped in a few leather shops and found some really good prices – surprisingly lower than in Florence. I couldn't figure it out: cheaper rent? Fewer tourists? Whatever the reason, if you're in Florence and planning on going to San Gimignano, hold out for your purchases! Lili got a nice purse for about half the price we had seen in Florence, and I saw a leather satchel of comparable quality (and I know my leather satchels) for a good 30% less.

We wandered up and down the street for a while longer, stopping in the Piazza della Cisterna to admire the vine-covered buildings and started discussing dinner plans. By now the crowds had really thinned out, although the shops were still open, making it quite pleasant and bright.

Seven of us were for eating here in Saint Jimmy, but Andrea wanted to get an even larger group together back in Florence...much to our dismay. Since he was driving (and since he never listens) we ended up stuck in traffic for an hour, hungry and irritated, on our way to yet another pizzeria with higher prices than this attractive little town.

Reflecting back on the day, I wondered if the visit to San Gimignano had been worth the drive — all things considered. If I could do it again, I decided that I would choose between Saint Jimmy and Greve or Lucca and Pisa. Both pairs are about an hour from Florence and are worth seeing. I wouldn't have killed myself on a tight schedule to see them all, though. If I had to choose, I give San Gimignano a miss just for the swarms of tourists you have to contend with there, despite the towers. After all, Lucca has some impressive towers, too.

Modena

Saving the first for last, a few words on Modena. Modena is a truly Italian city: it hardly feels like a city, but it has a cathedral so technically it is and it is considered a wealthy one, although the casual observer would be hard-pressed to find evidence of that (this is due, in part, to Italy's centuries-old tax laws). On a weekend, most of the population of Modena can be seen (and comes to be seen) along the arcaded Via Emilia and in the main square, the Piazza Grande, behind the Romanesque duomo. The most popular time to be here is Sunday evenings, dressed in one's Sunday best. The shops are open, the cafes are bustling, and the streets are packed with fashionable citizens wearing fashionable clothing, talking on fashionable cellphones and talking fashionable conversation. You would think that the frigid, humid winter would put people off, but no – we found the natives out in force as much during the biting cold winter weather as during the summer, albeit in furs, instead of halter tops.

To be honest, the Via Emilia through the center of town is quite pleasant and attractive, if not large or varied. The shopping is quaint, if not varied. We often found ourselves in the Café dell'Orologio, between the Via Emilia and the Piazza until the reopening of the grand Café Concerto right on the Piazza, which, despite its appallingly poor service, was a huge draw. As you might suspect, the building housing the café was quite old, but with its high vaulted ceilings, it was well-suited to a modern, buzzing café/restaurant. The large, outdoor patio (illegally reaching onto the piazza, but who's counting?) was quieter, and cooler. Surprisingly, the cappuccinos here were decently priced, if you could flag down a server to bring one.

The Piazza Grande (the name is relative to the other squares in Modena) is the center of the town – sorry, city – with arcaded walkways and the city's oldest buildings around it. Through the year, several events are held here, including a surprisingly authentic medieval fair, a great exotic car show – although in Modena they're local, not exotic, and of course the traditional Christmas celebration. Also of note was the ultra-low cost Internet access in the Palazzo Comunale, right on the piazza in the same room as the tourist information.

The duomo and the piazza are world-famous and are recognized by UNESCO as part of the patrimony of humanity. The duomo is an amazing place, even more so because it is still in use as a place of worship today. Begun in 1099, it was the first piece of architecture to be considered Romanesque. Although other churches are more impressive in size and scope, being first is quite an accomplishment. My favorite part (aside from the patron saint – more on that below) is the carved lions below the raised pulpit. They are rather grotesque, depicted eating knights and more. Touch them, if you can.

Before getting to the saint, I am reminded that the façade is covered with selected pictures from Genesis. After all, 1000 years ago very few people could read, so they relied on pictures to learn biblical stories. The most famous Old Testament stories, therefore, are depicted here for the education of the churchgoers.

And now, for my favorite part: it turns out the patron saint of Modena, San Gimignano (the same man as the town above), is in the cathedral crypt. He is kept in a rough-hewn stone coffin, which is closed except for his saint day, when he is uncovered for all to see…what's left of him, anyway. In life, some 1400 years ago, he was a short bishop, and death has not made him any larger. At this point, he is an incomplete skeleton (a lot of pieces had been parted out earlier) draped in a bishop's robe and miter.

A large procession goes through the crypt to touch the glass over him with hands or lips or items to be blessed. There is the usual complement of curlicues and objets d'art on the walls, as well, meaning there's no reason to be bored during church services.

Modena was, for some centuries, the capital of the Este dukes. They built an impressively large castle a few blocks from the duomo (with a direct path to their private door, of course). Today, the castle is the home of the military officers' school, which specializes in snappy, colorful uniforms.

Most people know Modena for a few other things: namely, food and cars. Modena is the birthplace of tortellini and balsamic vinegar, as well as the major production center of parmesan cheese and Parma ham. Being the capital of Emilia Romagna, the bread basket of Italy, there are plenty of fresh vegetables, squash, and lots of pork.

Other people know Modena as the home of Ferrari, Maserati, Lamborghini, DeTomaso, Zonda, and Pagani cars. Fiat also makes farm vehicles here. All in all, it's a mecca for car lovers, and the latest cars are always accessible for those with connections and brought out annually for a special event while classic cars are on display at the company museums.

Luciano Pavarotti is also from Modena, and gave his Pavarotti and friends concerts here every year. The locals knew that you could hear the concert quite well from a café outside the arena, which was a huge help when they would pause for commercial breaks after every song. If you want a taste of Pavarotti today, you can visit his family restaurant, Europa 92, just outside of town.

Which brings me to food: the overwhelming majority of the restaurants in Modena are purely traditional, local Italian. Meaning, they all serve pretty much the same food: tortellini, grilled vegetables, and pork. Pizza, the other staple, is available in just about every corner in Modena. The idea in Italian cuisine is that the more traditional, the better, and each restaurant tries to out-tradition the rest...which means they all taste pretty much the same. While it was tasty at first, the lack of variety eventually got to us. Again, many of the more traditional restaurants don't even have menus, so know what you like before you enter.

If Modena sounds like a great place to visit, with its location a mere half hour from Bologna and a couple of hours from Milan or Florence, it is. I wouldn't want to live here, but it's uncrowded and small, meaning you can do whatever you want without lines and you can do it all in a short stay.

Last Words

Looking back on our year in Italy, it was an enchanting place to spend time. The cities and towns were great fun to visit, with their similarities and differences, with their pizzas, piazzas and churches. The driving was a thrill and the people were...well, they were Italian – outgoing, boisterous, fiercely proud of their city, country, food and traditions. Italy is a wonderful place to visit, and I hope you love it and come back with great stories to tell. Ciao!

Made in the USA
Charleston, SC
16 May 2010